Advance Praise fc

Passages through Pakistan tells childhood as a 'third-culture kid', raised by her Christian, American missionary parents in the heart of Pakistan. Gardner's eloquent story of the trials, tribulations, and lessons of growing up as a bridge between these rich cultures serves as an important lens through which Americans and Pakistanis can learn more about one another and their important long-term partnership in a time when the gap between the two nations seems to be growing ever larger. By shedding light on how our faiths, our cultures, and our worlds are far more alike than different, Gardner's story is a must read for those wanting to build bridges.

~Ambassador Akbar Ahmed, Ibn Khaldun Chair of Islamic Studies, American University, Washington, DC

Marilyn Gardner's *Passages Through Pakistan* is a wonderful book, presenting in both a descriptive and reflective way the wonder of her childhood that took place in the mountains of northern Pakistan, the villages and deserts of southern Pakistan and the small towns of New England, along with some of the places in between.

As the only daughter in a remarkable family that included four brothers, Marilyn emerges as a sensitive observer with an impressive eye for detail as well as a well developed memory for the small anecdote that often reveals a much larger meaning.

Part spiritual reflection, part childhood reminiscence and part travelogue, Marilyn's book will be especially welcomed by those trying to make sense of their own personal stories, especially if they involve transitions across multiple cultures and geographic locations.

A deeply moving observer of the places, people and events that have surrounded her, she demonstrates sensitivity and understanding toward an often misunderstood part of the world, presenting the sights, sounds, landscapes and peoples of Pakistan in ways that are largely absent in both newspaper headlines and superficial social media accounts that all too often know little and understand even less.

Americans growing up in Asia and Asians growing up in America will especially gravitate toward this account, capturing as it does the complexity as well as the wonder and astonishment of childhoods spent in unlikely places. It will also resonate strongly with missionary kids and third culture kids everywhere.

~ Jonathan Addleton, former US Ambassador to Mongolia, is the author of several books including The Dust of Kandahar *and* Some Far and Distant Place

It's been said that if you dig down into your story deep enough, you find the common things. I didn't grow up in Pakistan, and I didn't experience boarding school or life as a missionary kid. But that doesn't matter, because in this book Marilyn digs down deep enough into her own journey that I found myself resonating throughout. And crying.

The cross-cultural connections and the cross-cultural stretching, the faith struggles, the reverence of older missionaries, the questions about God's sovereignty in the midst of catastrophe, and the confusion surrounding the loaded word, Calling. It's all here.

We need this story. The missions community needs this story. Yes, it's one person's history, but this is a book that missionaries and TCKs of all stripes need to read, because Passages through Pakistan ties us to our shared history. It links us with the bigger Story, and it reminds young cross-cultural workers that they're not the first. Not the first to travel. Not the first to care about social justice. Not the first to raise children abroad. It shows us that we are part of a larger plot arc that both preceded us and will in fact follow us. These reminders are much needed and deeply enriching.

I am sure that Marilyn's gentle storytelling and textured memories will encourage, inspire, and heal many.

~Jonathan Trotter, co-author of A-41: Essays on life and ministry abroad, *International Pastoral Counselor and contributor at the blog* A Life Overseas

For anyone who has wrestled with heavy bouts of homesickness or lived through long stretches of loneliness, Marilyn Gardner's new book, *Passages Through Pakistan*, is a gift.

For anyone who has walked through the valley of the shadow of death or of betrayal while simultaneously trying to hold onto faith in a good and loving God, this book is a light in your darkness.

For anyone who longs for the people and places of your past or has ever had to pack up a life and say goodbye, this book is a trustworthy traveling companion.

For anyone who has ever grappled seriously with their privilege or come face to face with their own shortcomings, this book is a safe place to land.

And for anyone who's ever wondered if it's even possible to raise a happy family in difficult or unusual circumstances, Passages Through Pakistan offers hope and, what's better, guidance.

But these stories are also a sober reminder to parents that no matter how much love and security we lavish upon our children, we cannot protect them from the sorrows and difficulties of this life – nor is it our job.

Marilyn's book is a gem for all these reasons, and it is also a joy to read. The language is beautiful, and each story is seasoned with profound truths about life and faith. Somehow as we read, we are able to swallow the bitter along with the sweet. That is what grace is all about, and that is what this book is all about.

~Elizabeth Trotter, co-author of A-41: Essays on life and ministry abroad,
Writer and editor at the blog A Life Overseas

Passages Through Pakistan

An American Girl's Journey of Faith

by Marilyn R. Gardner

Doorlight Publications
www.doorlightpublications.com

Copyright ©2017 Marilyn R. Gardner
Cover photo used with permission by Ralph and Pauline Brown

First published 2017 by Doorlight Publications.

ISBN 0-9838653-9- 1
ISBN13 978-0-9838653-9-1

Design & Production by Ruth Anne Burke

DOORLIGHT PUBLICATIONS

To my brothers
who have loved me well,
in Pakistan and beyond.

The train rounds a bend.
The rest of the cars appear
one by one,
all tied to one another
far into the distance
It comes as a surprise
to be tied to things so far back

Nazım Hikmet,
Human Landscapes from My Country

Contents

FOREWORD

THIS BOOK IS about growing up and about Pakistan and about faith. These three, intertwined, are my story.

I hold a special place in my heart for the country of Pakistan. I should – she nurtured me from three months to 18 years with few gaps in between. As I write this book, I am conscious of how little I really know about this beautiful and complex nation. I would be remiss if I did not acknowledge her complexity at the beginning.

Since 2009, Pakistan has been victim to more terrorist attacks than I am able to count. Bombs have gone off in markets, at churches, during volleyball games, during Friday prayers, at shrines, in neighborhoods, and even during funerals. The number of lives lost and the number of tragedies are unthinkable.

Yet the world still sits by and considers regular Pakistanis–who go about their lives working to support their families, educate their children, and live in peace – as suspect. So if in some small way this book humanizes Pakistan, then I will be satisfied. If in some small way this book can bring honor to this country, then I will be even happier.

THE TERM 'THIRD culture kid' was first developed in the 1960s by Dr. Ruth Useem. Dr. Useem was a sociologist and an anthropologist who introduced the concept of the 'third culture kid' after observing common characteristics of children who spent a significant amount of time growing up in a culture outside of their ancestral culture due to their parents' careers.

When you grow up between worlds, the research on identity formation does not apply in the same way. Instead, you move back and forth as one whose identity is being forged and shaped between two often conflicting cultures. "A British child taking toddling steps on foreign soil or speaking his or her first words in Chinese with an amah (nanny) has no idea of what it means to be human yet, let alone 'British.' He or she simply responds to what is happening in the moment" (Pollock and Van Reken, 2001).

Sometimes you fit into both worlds easily; other times fitting into one or the other is like wearing a pair of ill-fitting shoes that cause blisters and sores until you can't wait to take them off.

While I was growing up, the term 'third culture kid'"was not used and little was known about these children. I am grateful that this term is now part of the vocabulary of expatriates and that there is now a body of research devoted to the study of third culture kids.

The definition of the 'third culture kid' gave me a context and a reference point, a perspective that helped me understand myself better and, in so doing, better relate to others. Without this understanding, my story would be incomplete.

"A Third Culture Kid (TCK) is a person who has spent a significant part of his or her developmental years outside the parents' culture. The TCK frequently builds

relationships to all of the cultures, while not having full ownership in any. Although elements from each culture may be assimilated into the TCK's life experience, the sense of belonging is in relationship to others of similar background."

David Pollock, *Among Worlds*

There is a group of us who bear no identifying marks. We don't have the same accent, we don't pronounce or even necessarily spell words the same way. We can't tell one another at first glance. We don't wear the "home team" t-shirt.

But when we meet, it's like we're from the same place. We greet each other, we carry on, we tell stories, and we laugh wholeheartedly. It doesn't matter the age difference, the nationality, the gender. We connect.

Robynn Bliss, *Expectations and Burnout*

As you grow older, you have an expectation that you will fit into both worlds equally well, when in actual fact you fit into neither perfectly. Instead, you develop relationships and connections to both.

As WITH ANY major writing endeavor, there are so many people to thank. My editors – Dan Brown & Ruth Anne Burke – who kept me on track and took a meandering set of writings and turned it into an actual book, I cannot thank them enough; my parents whose choices gave me Pakistan; my brothers who shared so many of the same stories; and my extended family at Murree Christian School. As in any extended family, I have my favorites. Any of them could write their own book, and while some things would be similar, each of us have our unique memories that shaped who we have become. Special thanks to my aunties and uncles from various mission organizations. Some are no longer alive, but others continue to amaze me with their sheer joy and faithfulness in living. Special thanks to Auntie Betty, who has encouraged my writing from the start. Some Pakistanis may never know I wrote this book – Arbab, Martha Domji, Jamila – yet I think about them almost daily and I am so grateful for their impact on my life. A huge thank you to Ambassador Jonathan Addleton, someone I am proud to call my friend, for reading and commenting on the manuscript.

All my love and thanks goes to my husband Cliff. Not a day goes by without him encouraging me to write, write, and write some more. He is my soulmate and encourager and I could not be more grateful.

Lastly to Pakistan, Land of the Pure – thank you for your never-ending hospitality, your beauty, and your love. May God protect you and may you know peace.

Pakistan Zindabad.
(Long live Pakistan)

PROLOGUE

"My Country
I don't have any caps left made back home
Nor any shoes that trod your roads
I've worn out your last shirt quite long ago
It was of Şile cloth
Now you only remain in the whiteness of my hair
Intact in my heart
Now you only remain in the whiteness of my hair
In the lines of my forehead
My country"

Nazım Hikmet, *Human Landscapes from My Country*

In October of 2010 I went to Pakistan to work with people internally displaced by floods that had devastated much of the country. I had grown up in Pakistan, was nurtured on her soil, took my first steps and said my first words there. Pakistan was a land that knew me before I had a recollection of 'being', before I knew I was human. To return was a gift. My sister-in-law and I arrived in Karachi in the wee hours of the morning, exhausted by over twenty hours of travel. But I knew I was home. Every bone in my body felt it.

The two weeks that followed were full, hard, and glorious. We dispensed medicine out of the trunk of a van, drank *chai* made with unpasteurized buffalo milk, cried with the wounded, laughed at language mistakes, stopped to pick up fresh *pakoras* (vegetables deep fried in spicy batter) in the bazaar, and ate meals of hot, spicy curry while reminiscing with friends. Every day brought incredible joy. I was home.

On the last day of the trip, I made plans to visit an old friend. I had known Arbab in high school, and I loved her deeply, even as I acknowledged a monumental gulf between our worlds.

I waited at the front of the hospital compound, my hair held back in a short ponytail, a sky blue *dupatta* (light cotton scarf) over my head. The guard at the front gate had gone to fetch a motorized rickshaw to take us to Arbab's house. My heart beat fast, my foot tapped impatiently. As I waited I stood with a doctor, a gifted surgeon. She was new to Pakistan and struggling with the cultural disconnect that so often comes when West meets East.

"I remember running around the foundation of these buildings when I was a girl," I smiled as I remembered.

She looked at me, measuring her words. "A compound like this must have made life as a child in Pakistan at least somewhat bearable" she said.

I stood still and stared at her in shock. Bearable? Bearable? I repeated the word to myself. I said it aloud. "Bearable? It was more than bearable. My childhood was extraordinary."

In that moment my life made sense. I could see my childhood in Pakistan, years of disconnect in the United States, life as an adult back in Pakistan and then in Egypt, and finally my return to the United States as a stranger, an alien who had to learn to live, learn to belong.

In that moment, like Thornton Wilder's Emily, I was poised above the earth looking down at myself, my life in full. Suspended above the earth looking down at the scene, it all fit. The puzzle was complete. Like Emily, I got to go back:

> *"I didn't realize. All that was going on in life and we never noticed. Take me back – up the hill – Wait! One more look. Good-by, Good-by. Good-by, Oh, earth, you're too wonderful for anybody to realize you. Do any human beings ever realize life while they live it? – every, every minute?"*
>
> Thornton Wilder, *Our Town*

This was my story, a story written by the master storyteller, the author of life. Suddenly it all made sense. All the pain, all the joy, all the tears, and all the laughter, all of it. It all had meaning like I had never imagined. God himself orchestrated the journey I had traveled since birth. I was in awe and wordlessly gave thanks.

Chapter 1
Ocean Voyages

She watched the gap between ship and shore grow to a huge gulf. Perhaps this was a little like dying, the departed no longer visible to the others, yet both still existed, Only in different worlds

Susan Wiggs, *The Charm School*

I WAS CONCEIVED, I am told, on the Queen Mary. That once-majestic ship is now retired, forever docked in the blue-green waters of the Pacific near Los Angeles. In May of 1959 my parents were aboard the Queen Mary with their three older children – all boys. The four-week journey from Karachi to New York had its share of adventures. From my present vantage point, my conception is the most notable of them. I began in a tiny compartment, on a massive ship that rocked on the ocean waves.

Prior to World War II, the Queen Mary was known for her elegance. Originally labelled Job #534, she "captured hearts on both sides of the Atlantic." On her maiden voyage in 1936 she sailed from Southampton to Cherbourg and then across the Atlantic to the New York Harbor. She was massive, with dining halls, ballrooms, swimming pools, and even a squash court. The Queen proudly took the wealthy back and forth between countries and continents.

Then war came. During World War II the Queen Mary was put to utilitarian use as a troop transport. Stripped of the opulence that had made her so popular and painted a camouflage grey, she was fast and stealthy. A postwar rehabilitation brought the Queen back to the seas as a commercial ocean liner, and for over twenty years she continued her journeys back and forth across the seas. Along with the wealthy, she now took missionaries to their destinations far from the comfort of their homes in the Western Hemisphere.

When I was seven years old, the Queen Mary made her final voyage, docking in Long Beach. A ten-year-old photograph shows my three oldest children in Southern California with the great liner in the background. My husband sent the photo to my parents with a note. "If it hadn't been for you, these three wouldn't be here."

My family had begun the journey at Karachi Harbor, embarking on a much-needed furlough. Pakistan had become their adopted home seven years before, and during that time they had only been back to the United States once. Until the mid 1960s, my parents always traveled by ship. Air travel was expensive, reserved for the wealthy; sea travel was more economical. There was something wonderful about those six-week journeys, Mom once remarked, wistfully. They provided time and space to acclimate oneself, to adapt while slowly moving away from one country and, equally slowly, entering another. It was a floating world between two worlds, without expectation from or connection to either. Long days and nights alternated in slow rhythm, allowing my parents to rest and rejuvenate before arriving at the bustling harbor in Ellis Island.

My parents traveled during the golden years of the Queen Mary. They offered, I imagine, a stark contrast to their fellow passengers. Mom began her first book, *Jars of Clay*, with an anecdote from their first voyage to Pakistan in 1954. Listening to their shortwave radio one evening, they heard a familiar voice: *"I take missionaries out and bring monkeys back, and I don't know which is worse!"* It was the captain of the ship. As missionaries with a growing family, they were worlds apart from this captain and from the luxury passengers who later traveled with them on the Queen Mary. Everyone knew it.

My passage through Pakistan began here, in an elegant boat on a vast ocean, with long days at sea, and nights spread with stars in an expansive sky. I wish I could travel in time to witness the journey. During those long days and nights at sea, life happened. I happened. And somehow that was no accident.

ALTHOUGH I WAS conceived on a queen of the seas, I entered the world in a more ordinary place and time, in January, when Massachusetts is bitter cold, and snow falls heavy on the bare maples and oaks. A New England January is barren and bleak. The only warmth is inside beside a fire. I still hate the cold.

I was born in Winchendon, a factory town in North-Central Massachusetts. A giant rocking horse, painted white and red, sits on Winchendon's town common, a reminder of days when the town was a bustling toy-making hub. The original rocking horse, Clyde, created by one of the owners of the Converse Toy & Woodenware Company, is the town's icon.

Three baby girls were born that last week of January in the small town hospital. I was one of them. Those who may wish to make pilgrimage to the scene of such an important event are out of luck. The hospital did not survive past the seventies when it was overtaken by larger, more sophisticated medical centers in nearby cities. As the first baby girl in a family with three lively boys, I was, without doubt, the Princess. My place in this family was unassailable, and throughout my childhood I knew it.

Winchendon was Mom's hometown. My maternal grandparents, Stanley and Cyrena Ruth Kolodinski, had four children: Pauline, my mom; twins, Bill and Charlotte; and Jean, a blonde, blue-eyed beauty with a personality to match. My grandmother, known affectionately as "Grandma K" to most everyone, was a gentle, unassuming woman. She had survived a broken heart after my grandfather died of a heart attack when he was 50 years old. She grieved with grace. "They say that time heals these wounds," Grandma K said to me one day, "but I miss your Grandpa Stanley more now than I did the day after he died." It was a powerful, unforgettable lesson on grief.

Mom was smart. Few children from Winchendon went to college but she was determined that she would. Her Polish-Lithuanian father, who had come through Ellis Island as a child, was dismissive. "What do girls need with college?" he said. She was undeterred. At mom's college graduation, her dad was the proudest man in the room.

But a more decisive change had already happened many years earlier. A tall gentleman with a deep Swedish accent came to Winchendon's small Baptist church when Mom was a child. He spoke about mission work in India, and Mom's heart was stirred. That night she decided to do everything she could to become a missionary.

Dad's family was also from Western Massachusetts. Ralph Edward Brown was the fourth child and only son of Annie and Edward Utley Brown, my paternal grandparents. His mother, Annie, struggled to nurse him; he seemed unable to take either breast milk or regular formula and he failed to thrive. The milkman, aware of the problem, suggested sweetened condensed milk. Having nothing to lose, Annie diluted this in a bottle, and to everyone's astonishment, Ralph not only survived but thrived. To this day, he blames his love for sweet things on his early diet.

Tragedy struck when Dad was four. His father died during a hospitalization for a broken leg. Annie, left alone with five children and an empty space in her home and heart, raised the family with grit and grace during an era when life was not kind to a widow and her children. Dad recalls a community of friends and relatives, many from Morningside Baptist Church in Pittsfield, who walked alongside the family during this time.

Dad grew into a young man with a personality and character as large as his smile. After graduation he entered the Air Force, but to his disappointment instead of flying planes and braving enemy combatants, he spent his military career processing paperwork and filling out tedious forms in triplicate. Two years later, thanks to the GI bill, he enrolled at Gordon College on Boston's Fenway where he met his life-long love. Pauline evidently stole his heart after one or two "Joyces" and perhaps a "Ruthanne." He has never been completely clear on this. Undoubtedly, one of the things that attracted them to each other was their mutual desire to go overseas as foreign missionaries.

They were married in 1951, surrounded by mountain laurel and a host of family and friends attending and wishing them well. Almost immediately, they began planning their future overseas.

Mom and Dad welcomed their firstborn, my oldest brother, Edward Ralph, on March 16th, 1953, two years after they were married. A year-and-a-half later their lives dramatically changed when they boarded the Steel Recorder in New York Harbor to begin their voyage to Karachi.

A 50-year-old photograph shows Mom, wearing white gloves and pearl earrings, holding a baby in her arms. She is standing on the deck of a ship, a slight smile on her face, beautiful and shyly sophisticated, worlds away from the country where she would make her home for over 35 years. The photograph gives few clues of her resiliency, or the ability she would show to redirect her Yankee independence to fit cultural norms without ever losing a bit of spirit.

Dad became as accustomed to sitting cross-legged on the floor in a Marwari tribal village and relishing onion curry as he was preaching from the pulpit at Morningside Baptist and enjoying a potluck church supper. Mom learned to parse Sindhi verbs and decipher the nuances of language and culture. Veiled women became dear friends. Curry, and *chapatis*, became a staple. They learned to live, love, and make a home in desert towns extraordinarily different from Winchendon or Pittsfield where they were raised. When I was born, Mom and Dad had already established a life on both sides of the globe. They had a foot in both countries, and had learned to negotiate this space between two worlds.

Soon after my birth, my parents left from New York Harbor to begin the six-week ocean voyage back to Pakistan. Along with the still-lively three boys, they had a newborn in tow. This was my first full journey overseas. I am the baby in the faded black-and-white photograph. In my imagination, I see a young, vulnerable family on a huge ship in an ocean so vast they would go for days without seeing land. How did they do it? How did they nurture us and keep their hope and love alive? The answer is without doubt in their faith, a faith that had begun so many years before and continued to direct their decisions, both big and small

Our ship docked in the harbor at Karachi, Pakistan's busy port city. Karachi served as a useful stop prior to making the long rail journey to Ratodero, a small city where my parents made their home.

Karachi was a city of *gymkhanas*, large, palm-tree bordered roads, and sprawling villas. Along with that, the poor arrived daily from villages throughout Pakistan, and large slums emerged in various parts of the city. The distinct disparity between rich and poor was a reality that I was not aware of in childhood. I saw Karachi as a magical city – my favorite place to shop and vacation.

Our favorite grocery shopping area was the famed Empress Market, built during the British occupation. The market provided a number of shops where Mom could stock up on store-bought butter, meat, sugar, flour, and yeast to last the family at least three months. Travel was infrequent and not easy, so trips to Empress Market were important.

My memories of these early years are sometimes clouded, other times as vivid as the bright colors painted onto Pakistani trucks and buses. When I first arrived in Karachi the country was still young, born only 13 years earlier in 1947. In 1954 when my parents first arrived, Pakistan was raw with fresh memories of the violence and struggle of a difficult and precarious independence. Yet during my childhood, I would only partially grasp the challenging history of this country. My world was safe, cocooned by my parents' love and a sheltering community. I belonged. Pakistan was home. Anything outside of Pakistan was 'other.' I would not form memories of my country of birth and citizenship until much later.

MY EARLIEST MEMORY is from Ratodero, a small city located around 30 kilometers from Larkana. In the memory I am small, a preschooler, sitting on a bed on a rooftop, smiling beneath gauzy mosquito netting. A faded photograph confirms the image in my mind. I look at the camera. My older brother, Tommy, sitting on his bed beside mine, looks at me. We woke early on that rooftop, responding to the morning light and sounds of early morning – roosters, the call to prayer, oxen carrying heavy loads – that still evoke the joy of my childhood.

We were the only foreigners in the city, and we had the only car. Our house, where Bibles abounded and daily prayer was as important as daily bread, was surrounded on four sides by mosques. The call to prayer not only woke us in the morning, it was our melody at lunch, our call to afternoon tea, and the mournful, melancholy music of our evening hours. The high walls of the house guarded three courtyards at three different levels, giving us space to play and privacy from the many eyes curious to observe this white, foreign family. A trough that had at one time been used to water animals became our swimming pool in the hot months. We lived peaceful, noisy lives in this place.

This house, with its high ceilings and arched doors, was my first home. With it come memories of my dolls, my brothers, mosquito netting, early morning whispering –and a prized doctor set, perhaps my earliest achievement. I was a thumb sucker. Mom desperately wanted me to stop sucking my thumb so that parasites would stop entering my body. Determined to achieve this goal, she told me that if I could go a month without sucking my thumb she would give me a doctor set; a real, live, plastic doctor set. It would be white, with a red cross on the front. Inside would be plastic syringes, a thermometer, a stethoscope, along with fake bandages and eye patches. I had seen one of these before and I dreamed of having my own. The task was a difficult one, but I was stubborn. I wanted that doctor set.

Every day for thirty days I asked Mom about the set. I imagined giving my dolls shots and wound care. I wrapped make-believe bandages tightly across arms, legs, and naked torsos. I anticipated establishing a doll hospital, complete with injured dolls and beds made of boxes and old cloth. Mom, in her mercy, had determined that if I sucked my thumb at night it would not count. But every night, as she popped her head around my door to look at my tousled pixie hair rumpled on a pillow, she saw my thumb, just inches from my mouth, but never in.

On day thirty, I was declared the winner. I got my doctor set, and my imaginary play rose to new heights. It also foreshadowed the future. I went on to become a nurse with real bandages, stethoscopes, and syringes, and my patients would no longer be a motley set of dolls, but real people who hurt, bled, and sometimes died. Mom still tells this story with admiration and amazement in her eyes.

Why do some memories stay while others fade? Is it because the memory is so important to those close to us that they continually remind us, perhaps realizing that if it is not passed on then one of their memories, a family narrative, will die? Did Mom tell me this to pass on family history, or was it more than that? We are marked by stories from our childhood, our personalities linked and shaped by the narratives we are told. These memories of others become our stories and stay with us, even when they are old and faded. As life grows more complicated, we return to these stories to remember, to remind ourselves who we are. Remembering builds strength and resilience. The story established itself in my memory because it was bigger than a strong-willed little girl determined to get her prize. It told me who I was.

Research shows that a determining factor in the emotional health and resilience in a child is the knowledge that she is part of a bigger story. My stories and memories from Ratodero are gleaned from tattered pictures and from Mom and Dad. I was too young to remember most of them. But these small narratives place me within a larger family narrative, a narrative written on both sides of the globe with thousands of stories contributing to the whole. The story stubbornly continues through the years, determined to go on – like a four-year-old who stops sucking her thumb, single-minded and intent on a prize, determined to get the doctor set with its bright red cross emblazoned on the white exterior.

ONE OF THE most powerful and poignant stories in our family's narrative comes from a Christmas when I was three years old, living in Ratodero. The city, with its dusty streets, flat-roofed houses with courtyards, and donkeys and ox carts that brayed and roamed outside, resembled ancient Bethlehem more than anywhere Mom or Dad had ever been.

Despite the biblical setting, adjusting to Christmas in Pakistan was a challenge. Loneliness and homesickness tended to descend on my parents like thick clouds during the holidays, made more difficult by their desire to create magic for their children. They were acutely aware of the absence of grandparents and other extended family members back in the U.S. During one particular Christmas Mom felt that it was more than she could bear. She felt more than ever like we were "deprived" of a "real" Christmas.

A few days before Christmas, after we were put to bed, Mom went up on the roof top. As she looked out over the city of Ratodero, the tears she had been holding back for our sake began to fall. She was a world removed from the Christmases of her past. There was no extended family, no white-steepled church, no lights on Main Street. As she watched the bright stars, millions of light years away, she heard singing just as the shepherds heard singing on that night so long ago. Could it be angels? It was a moment of wonder and awe that the God whom she loved so deeply would provide angels to bring comfort and a reminder that she was not alone.

There were no heavenly angels, but "earth angels" had arrived in the form of our dear friends, the Addletons and the Johnsons – two missionary families with seven kids between them. Out of love for our family they had traveled along a bumpy, dusty road, remembering that we were alone in this city. Once there they stood in the street outside our front door singing "Joy to the World, the Lord is Come. Let Earth receive Her King!" They celebrated with cups of hot cocoa and frosted sugar cookies before heading back into the night. Through the years we have told the story of these "angels from the rooftops" over and over, one more story in the larger family narrative.

LIFE IN SINDH seemed far from the broader national politics of Pakistan. Sindh was in the south and, though much of it was desert, fertile ground by the Indus River allowed for farming. In the 1900s barrages and canals were built that allowed better farming for Sindhis. Punjabis in the north occupied the corridors of power. Sindhis, a minority group both in population and geography, were often marginalized. And Sindh was hot. People who lived there bore the marks of a heat that wears down the body. They often exhibited a striking patience and acceptance of all of life, an acceptance that I also learned. Sitting on *charpais* (rope beds) in the hot sun makes you sanguine and not easily disturbed. Flies landed and lounged on our heads, aiming for the eyes and the lips if we did not fan them away. We learned to sit for hours on *charpais*, in sweltering church services, and in hot cars. Sindhis had a humor and good will that extended to those of us who were their guests. My gregarious father fit in perfectly. A photographer in Shikarpur once captured his photo, enlarged it, and prominently displayed it in his shop at the entrance of the Shikarpur bazaar so the entire community could see. Dad was "Brown Sahib" of the white hair and smile as big as his heart. His picture gazed on all who entered the area, ever looking out on a land and people that he had come to love.

We moved from town to town during my childhood, but I was unfazed. My constants were my boarding school, based in a solid stone building in Murree, and my parents, who, though flesh and blood, seemed equally solid and immoveable. Pakistan was home. She adopted me, a foreigner, and took me in. I belonged. I belonged in the family and in the community into which I was born. I belonged in the country where I took my first steps. Legal documents might say otherwise, but they were unimportant to the reality of my experience.

I learned early on of the beauty and hospitality of Pakistan. My eyes captured landscapes that the best photographers in the world could not capture, and the music and colors are etched on my mind. I was welcomed into homes and churches, played in courtyards and on canal banks.

In my childhood, the Pakistan I knew was a place of color and life: bright oranges, reds, yellows, and greens of spices and fabrics. I knew the ready invitations to come for tea that brought smiles to my face and delight to my heart. I knew the best food in the world – mouthwatering and piping hot *pakoras*; kebabs purchased in the middle of the bazaar in the afternoon; spicy, red-orange, charred chicken *tikka* with *naan* and fresh lemon; the cold tang of lemon squash; and chicken *masala*'s thick, onion-filled sauce that made my nose run through an entire meal. The tastes and spices lingered long after the meal was over. I knew Pakistan as a place of food, music, colors, and laughter.

This was my home, the setting of my earliest memories, my first steps, my first kiss, my first love. I literally cut my first teeth in this land. Pakistan was a place of life and faith. I was surrounded by Pakistanis who loved me and put up with the immaturity of my childhood. This was where my physical and faith journey began. Would I ever love another place so much? I didn't think so.

Later, I would come to know the complexity and contradiction that defined this homeland that had adopted me, but in early years I knew only the good. I would later discover more of her history. I would learn of a Pakistan birthed in violence and tragedy, a land that continues to face crisis after crisis – some at the hands of other governments, and some of its own making. I would learn of the difficulty of a country that struggled to find her identity apart from the larger Indian subcontinent. I would see the struggles in my friends around marriage and family and learn of the massive disparities between the wealthy and the poor. Later, I would learn that in addition to the beauty of friendship and hospitality there was also the horror of violent fundamentalism. I would be introduced to and angered by the one-dimensional Pakistan of Western perception and media. I would understand that alongside stunning landscapes of high mountains and clear lakes was the dirt and raw sewage of cities. I would later face disease, high infant morbidity and mortality, inescapable poverty, and the light hair and big bellies of malnutrition. I would grow to see many dimensions of this beautiful, complex land.

But the Pakistan of early childhood was a beautiful home, and I loved that home.

My earliest memories are in Ratodero, but Jacobabad is the place I associate most strongly with my earliest years. Jacobabad was founded in the 1800s by a British general, General John Jacob. General Jacob was known for doing a great deal to help the city, and while many other cities bearing the names of British elite were renamed, the residents of

Jacobabad refused to change the name. General Jacob was buried in the city and left a large Victorian clock tower in the center that stands to this day. Jacobabad consistently recorded some of the hottest temperatures in the subcontinent. With summer temperatures soaring to 48 degrees Celsius and beyond, it is easy to see why people are relaxed. Jacobabad is so hot that it's difficult to get excited or angry about anything.

We moved to Jacobabad when I was five, and at our house there I remember Mom's first attempts at gardening. Her native Massachusetts was full of vibrant colors that characterized the four seasons. The climate of Sindh – the heat, the lack of foliage, the desert plants, the unknown seasons – none of it was familiar. Mom was desperate for some color in the clay that surrounded our house. While bougainvillea and desert plants survived and brought with them flashes of color, there was nothing that compared to the variety and vibrancy of the plant life of her Massachusetts home. After failed attempts at planting flowers, she finally gave up and placed some fake flowers in flowerbeds surrounding the house. We were all delighted with the outcome. Bright spots of yellow, purple, fuchsia, blue, and green radiated against the mud-colored brick of our home. From far away they looked real. That was good enough for us.

Others around us were equally pleased. Only hours after they were planted, the flowers disappeared. We were deeply disappointed, angry that someone would steal our flowers. This was our home, our yard, our haven, and a thief had violated our space. I don't remember Mom's reaction. I can guess that she was disappointed and angry, perhaps tearful. Mom missed her home more than she could possibly articulate, especially to her children who would not understand the loneliness of living in an alien land until they were older. But that is her story. My story is one of childish indignation and hurt. It was my earliest experience of betrayal. Who would do this to us? I thought we were loved. When you're loved, people don't steal your flowers.

I was a headstrong little girl, stubborn and sassy. I suffered for my independence in various ways – at five a broken bone, at six my mouth washed out with soap for talking back to Mom and Dad, at seven a spanking for sticking out my tongue at Pakistani friends. The broken bone was the most traumatic; sticking out my tongue would provide the best life lesson.

The afternoon that I broke my leg, I had been sent to the top of my bunk bed as punishment for some now-forgotten offense. After granting me the allotted time to reflect on my actions, Mom called me to the kitchen, and I threw myself off my bed in anger at the perceived injustice. My anger immediately dissolved into tears of pain, and I was immediately sorry for my naughtiness. From my howls of pain and inability to walk, my parents knew this was more than a small sprain. But Jacobabad was a three-hour drive from a mission hospital in the city of Sukkur. The trip would have to wait for the morning.

That night I woke up intermittently to deep pain and to the sound of Mom's beautiful voice reading from Patricia St. John's *Rainbow Garden*. She read about a bratty young protagonist, Elaine, who broke her leg and ended up spending the night with a criminal. Hearing the story of Elaine, how she survived her trauma, and how she came out on the other side, at peace with both God and the people around her, made my accident seem like it would yield something worthy. Even at five, I identified with characters in books, and the story seemed uncanny in resemblance to my situation.

We left for Sukkur the next morning. I saw the doctor and ended up with a thigh-high cast. Along with providing a canvas for autographs and artistic endeavors, it was also my passport to empathy, a respite from the regular good-hearted teasing of my brothers.

Other events in Jacobabad show how dependent we were on each other and on friends from afar. At one point, Dad was traveling while Mom stayed at home with my little brother Dan and me. My older brothers were away at boarding school, and we were the only foreigners in the city. All three of us spiked high fevers. Mom tried desperately to cope, but grew increasingly anxious about her ability to look after two little ones while being so sick herself. There were no telephones, and we didn't travel without a great deal of planning. If we needed help quickly, we used telegrams. Finally, realizing she could no longer carry on alone, Mom sent a telegram to friends in Shikarpur. "Ralph traveling. Stop. Kids and I very sick. Stop. Need help. Stop."

That same night, Auntie Betty and Uncle Ben Ralston arrived from Shikarpur, where they lived with their three boys. They had left as soon as they received the telegram asking for help. Wrapping us tightly in quilts, they put all three of us into their car and drove into the night toward the safety of community. Auntie Betty held me on her lap, tight and secure. I knew in that moment that more than anything I wanted to be held. The safety and security that were absent when we were alone, bodies broken by fever, had now arrived, and I never wanted to be let go. I remember thinking that I needed to scratch my nose, but if I wiggled free to scratch my nose, Auntie Betty might think I didn't want to be held. I couldn't risk it. So I remained still as Auntie Betty continued to hold me, oblivious to the internal struggle and my deep, human need for security. We drove through the dark night toward Shikarpur and the safe community of missionary aunties, uncles, and friends who would care for us.

Our community in Jacobabad was a small, struggling Christian church and school. Sunday mornings and evenings, the Christian community gathered, strong voices singing Punjabi hymns with enthusiasm. Events and hospitality were constant, whether it was tea with two or three, or large programs with hundreds of children. Sometimes Mom stayed at home with my little brother while Dad perched me on the bar of his bicycle to ride to the services. One Sunday I caught my foot in the spokes of the wheel. I screamed with pain as I looked down at torn skin and blood. Pakistanis immediately came to my aid, carrying me off the bike and holding me, speaking gentle phrases in Sindhi to comfort my tears as my father resituated himself. They were kind and considerate, deeply concerned for my welfare. Dad took me home, where my ankle received the attention of salve and bandages, the security and safety of love. Safety and love became the solid foundation for my childhood, always appearing when I needed them. Bad things might happen, but help would come, whether from Auntie Betty or Pakistani strangers. I would be cared for.

My attitude toward Pakistanis was not always noble, particularly in my early childhood. The hardest spanking I ever received was for sticking my tongue out at two Pakistani teenagers after church one day. My brothers and I were waiting in our car for our parents and, without parental supervision, I was enduring the teasing that only a girl growing up in a family of boys could imagine. Onlookers in the church yard found this understandably amusing, so I turned the wrath that meant nothing to my brothers onto the closest onlookers. Looking at them, I stuck out my tongue and put my fingers into my ears, waving my hands. It's a face that has been used by children through the centuries, but I immediately regretted my lapse in judgment. "We're telling!" shouted one or two of my brothers, and I dreaded what would come. The spanking I received that day a lesson I never forgot. My parents might not always understand their host culture, they might have their own frustrations with some of the cultural differences they daily encountered, but they always knew that they were guests. To have one of their children act so obnoxiously would not be tolerated. The spanking was a lesson in humility and respect, and I bore the sting of it for a long time. The lesson was unforgettable.

My childhood life was a blur of movement and change. We lived all over the Sindh desert – in Ratodero, Jacobabad, Larkana, Hyderabad, and Shikarpur. At four-year intervals we travelled to the United States, and every summer we packed our bags and moved our household to Murree.

Murree, where cool breezes blew through pine trees, and the ghosts of a past British military presence seem to swirl around the rafters of old churches and graveyards, is a resort town 7,000 feet above sea level. The town is located in the foothills of the Himalayan mountain region. On clear days you can see some of the highest, most spectacular mountains in the world. Murree's history as a mountain resort goes back to the 1800s. Until 1864, Murree was the summer capital of the Punjab Province of British India. When the hot weather became too much to bear and all one could do was sit under high ceilings with fans blowing hot air around the room, people with means would escape to Murree. The town had some noted visitors and residents. A British novelist, Berta Ruck, was born there and grew up to write several short stories and over 90 romance novels. Had I known that a British novelist lived in such close proximity to me, I would likely have dreamed of appearing as a character in one of her books, preferably a beautiful young woman with a dramatic and unrequited love.

The town's main mall area stretched from the post office perched on top of a hill, past the Holy Trinity Church, on down to St. Margaret's Church and gardens. Holy Trinity, built in 1857, marked the center of town and was the place of worship for British army officers in colonial days and for missionaries following Pakistan's independence. On sunny days, flower *wallahs* would sell beautiful blue irises and long-stemmed white lilies to Pakistani and foreign women alike. Small shops that sold bolts of bright-colored cloth, fragile bangles, and other goods lined the wide street. This was where I ate my first ice cream cone, had my first kiss, and discovered marijuana growing in the church yard of Holy Trinity. Murree was special.

Some of my early memories of our home in Murree are of blackened windows and early lights out. Until ten years ago, I had no idea why. I was in kindergarten and, although children are excellent recorders of events, they are often poor interpreters. My mind recorded the event, but I remembered only the impact on our lives. The 'why' was unimportant. Recently my husband, an excellent historian, became curious about what war had us in the grip of those precautions in 1965. It was the war was between India and Pakistan over the disputed Kashmir territory, which was just north of us. Pakistan sent military forces into Kashmir to challenge Indian occupation and enforce its claims. India responded with a full-scale attack on all of West Pakistan. The war lasted 17 days, ending with a cease-fire negotiated by the Soviet Union and the United States.

As a five-year-old child, I was blissfully ignorant of the turmoil that raged around us. What mattered was that we had cocoa and stories in Mom and Dad's bed during mandatory blackouts. The BBC radio with its catchy theme tune was on night and day as Mom and Dad anxiously listened for any news. Blackouts ended soon after the cease-fire, but the books and cocoa with the soundtrack of the BBC World Service were continuing features in our lives. Six years later, in 1971, when India and Pakistan went to war again, and East Pakistan became Bangladesh, the BBC was still a part of our family routine. I would not realize until much later the atrocities on both sides of this bloody, violent conflict, but the clipped accents of the BBC newscasters entered my psyche as familiar sounds of home and belonging. I would desperately miss these voices after I left home.

To my adult perspective, it is remarkable that in the midst of these events I was never afraid. Only my immediate world was important. Warplanes might fly overhead, and newscasters proclaim dire warnings, but my world was safe. Such is the beauty of a secure childhood.

FOR THE MISSIONARY family, 'furlough' had distinctive connotations quite unknown to Merriam-Webster, which defines a furlough as time away for soldiers, employees, or prisoners. For missionary families, furloughs involved reunion with family, a grueling schedule of church events, and the shock of how much we had changed while away from our passport countries. During the "furlough" year, we adopted a "normal" American life. We walked to day school, we packed school lunches, we participated in after-school events, and we attended church youth groups.

My parents' life in Pakistan came at a cost and that cost had names – Grandma K; Aunt Jean and Uncle Jim; their children; our cousins whose names all began with a first initial of J; Aunt Charlotte who would give us treat bags to last an entire sea voyage across the Atlantic Ocean; and my father's sisters – Aunt Lois, Aunt Edna, Aunt Ruth, and Aunt Gracia. Scattered from Tacoma, Washington, to Winchendon, Massachusetts, were many relatives with many names. There were also childhood friends and college soulmates. There was Mom's friend Joanne who had also given birth at the same hospital during the same cold January that I entered the world; and Dad's friend Doc Murdoch who regaled us with tales of Dad as a college student. All of these names became real to us during furlough years as Mom and Dad reconnected, introducing us to the world they had left.

Grandma K was one of the constants during our furlough years. It was during this time that she introduced her five 'foreign' grandchildren to the wonders of baseball, candlepin bowling, and Ritz crackers with peanut butter. While my parents would head off to churches, we would sit in Grandma K's small living room watching Red Sox games on her little black-and-white television. I like to believe it would delight her that I, her most unlikely granddaughter who grew up across the ocean, now live within walking distance of the great Fenway Park and avidly follow the Red Sox . Grandma K knew how to create a safe place for us during our furlough years.

Furloughs also meant church visits. Every four years I was reminded of the good folk who supported our family through tithing and more. Our family's financial livelihood depended on churches believing in what my parents were doing. My thoughts about these churches were not always gracious. I fashioned myself as superior, boasting greater knowledge of the world and more stamps in my passport than they had ever seen before. While in Pakistan, I was secure in family and community, but that identity was threatened in the strange new environment of furlough. I protected myself with an air of superiority, desperately trying to hold on to a sense of self. The result was arrogance.

That air of superiority was bolstered by minor celebrity status that included features in *The Worcester Telegram* or *The Winchendon Courier*, and supporting roles on stage at church missions conferences. In predominantly Roman Catholic New England, my parents were a novelty. Mom's hometown was perhaps grudgingly proud that one of their own had made it far beyond Winchendon to a land known only through a couple of paragraphs in social studies textbooks.

There was also pure magic in those early furloughs, especially at Christmas. Pakistani Christmases were wonderful expressions of a life between worlds. We draped lights and tinsel on desert shrubs, served hundreds of cups of tea to Pakistani guests who came to wish us a *Baradin mubarak* (Blessed Big Day,) participated in long and dramatic Christmas pageants, and woke to early-morning stockings. Christmases in America were completely different. Our New England white Christmases meant sledding in my cousins' back yard, "real" Christmas trees with sparkling lights, presents, and family and friends pouring into our lives with gifts and love. Of course these Christmases were magical.

On my first American Christmas, we lived in Aunt Jean and Uncle Jim's Hyde Park Street home in Winchendon. Grandma K had vacated her living quarters in the front of the house, making room for our family for the year. Behind the house Uncle Jim's land stretched back to 'Big Hill', a small hillock to those who were big, but a place of adventure – perfect for sledding, perfect for picnics – to us who were little. I was four that Christmas, and on Christmas morning I could barely contain my excitement. After the traditional stocking in Mom and Dad's bed, Dad and my Uncle Jim shut the door of the living room where we would open gifts together. "Is it time yet? Can we go in?" I remember none of the gifts, but I will never forget the magic of the wait.

Earlier in the season, Mom and I secretly decorated my grandmother's small apartment on Central Street with a tree and Christmas ornaments. We left before Grandma K returned home. Later I smiled a wide, gap-toothed smile as I stood on a chair listening on the telephone to Grandma's exclamations of delight and surprise. I understand now the emotions Mom must have felt at such times. These visits home to the place of her childhood, where white, fluffy snow dressed the sidewalks in winter and wildflowers grew in the summer, provided precious, fleeting opportunities to be with her mom and to introduce her children to her family and heritage. As a child, I could not know that the meaning of home would be different for me. Mom's roots would always be in Massachusetts, but Pakistan would become the place of my earliest memories, relationships, and faith formation. For my parents, furloughs were a respite and connection – a return home – that I could only later understand.

I FIND IT hard to look back on the faith of my childhood without making it more complicated than it actually was. Adult feelings and my adult journey overwhelm my childhood self. But faith was not complicated. Faith just was. From my infant dedication in a Baptist church in Massachusetts, faith was a part of my life, intertwined with my personhood and my sense of self. Faith was all around me. It was in my parent's decision to leave their home country. It was in the daily prayers we said in our home. Faith was in the church services we attended, in the people who became a part of our lives. And faith was not only present in Christians. An equally-strong faith surrounded us. The call to prayer clocked our comings and our goings, mosques were around every corner, greetings included the name of God, responses to invitations invoked the name of God. Faith was ever-present. It guided our lives and the lives of those around us.

Faith was "asking Jesus into my heart" when I was five years old. My younger brother Dan had tonsillitis. Mom, Dan, and I had traveled to Quetta, where he would have his tonsils taken out by a British surgeon. We stayed with missionary friends from New Zealand. I was in bed, tucked in tight after bedtime stories, songs, and prayer. But I couldn't sleep. First I was hungry, so Mom patiently brought me a small, sweet banana. Sleep eluded me.

When I disturbed Mom again, it wasn't about physical hunger. I told her I wanted to ask Jesus into my heart. We prayed a short prayer – a simple prayer that many have called the "salvation" prayer. I didn't know what it was called, but in my childish understanding, and as one who was already secure and beloved, sleep came quickly as my five-year old self rested in that prayer and in Jesus. I have no doubt that something happened that night. In my limited understanding of life and faith, I prayed a child's prayer, completely trusting and uncomplicated. That child's prayer set a foundation that would continue to grow in clarity – and in complexity.

Inseparable from this first concrete memory of faith formation is the memory of my mother, repeatedly returning to my room long after I should have been asleep. Perhaps this too – the patience of a mother in a child's spiritual journey – paved the way for a strong future faith that began so simply in childlike prayer.

Chapter 2
RAIL JOURNEYS

Railway termini are our gates to the glorious and the unknown. Through them we pass out into adventure and sunshine, to them, alas! we return.

E. M. Forster, *Howards End*

TRAIN TRAVEL IN Pakistan began on the 13ᵗʰ of May, 1861, when a 105-mile rail line joined Karachi to Kotri. Almost a century later, trains were part of the fabric of our lives; the Awami Express, the Bolan Mail, Karachi Express, and the Khyber Mail became household words. We spent hours on trains, hours waiting at stations, and hours traveling bumpy roads to and from the stations. Pakistan's railway system was central to the nation's commercial, educational, and social networks, and it still is. But trains were not always associated with progress. During the bloody partition of India, trains carrying mutilated bodies from both sides of the conflict steamed into Amritsar and Lahore, playing a gruesome role in the strife-filled beginning of the Land of the Pure.

Pakistani train stations are busy places, alive with *chai-wallahs* (tea vendors), vendors of hard-boiled eggs, stands selling hot *puris* (deep-fried flat bread) and *halwa* (a sweet, dense pudding), and hawkers of small paper cones filled with *channa dal* (lentil curry). Thousands of travelers make their way through train stations across the country, luggage and *bisters* (large canvas carriers stuffed with bedding) piled high around them as they wait. Families traveled together, the wealthy in first or air-conditioned class, the poor in cramped and crowded third class compartments. We experienced both, straddling the worlds of rich and poor.

Because we traveled the 800 miles to our boarding school by train, the train station became an emotion-laden place – a place of nervous dread and anticipation as I awaited the arrival of our train; a place of silent tears as I waved goodbye, through dirt-smudged windows; a place of relief and joy as I stepped out of the train that returned me to the waiting arms and hearts of my parents. The backdrop to all of these emotions was the sheer exhaustion of long days and nights of travel. The rhythmic sounds of the train, the smell of dust on fake leather seats, the noise and chaos of train stations, the high-pitched sounds of street vendors, and the smell of hot *puris* and *halwa* were all a part of childhood, sounds and smells seared into the memory.

Each journey's routine was the same. We waited on a crowded platform, surrounded by every imaginable size of bag, attracting a crowd of curious onlookers. Pale skin and strange speech immediately marked us as foreign. When the train finally pulled in, waiting gave way to a frantic flurry of people and luggage as we rushed to load our bags before the train pulled away from the station. Once the train arrived, it was almost impossible to say a proper goodbye; yet it was equally impossible to say goodbye before that. We were stuck in limbo, filled with a desire to speak, but tongue-tied until it was too late. Once aboard, the rhythm of the train overtook us, moving from ears and body to soul, poetic and lyrical, taking us farther, farther, and farther even as it brought us closer, closer, closer.

ONLY THREE YEARS ago, Mom made the startling observation that between ages six and 18 I had never slept in the same bed for more than three months. I was astonished. My internal restlessness and the impulse to rearrange furniture several times each year seemed to make better sense, validating what I had seen as a deficit. Mom's simple, matter-of-fact observation, like the rhythm of trains, evokes a recurring theme in my story.

Throughout my early years, I had been prepared for the day when I would leave for boarding school. I knew I would be leaving for the largely unknown – but exciting – world of boarding school. I knew that as soon as I was school age, I would join brothers and friends on the journey away from the Sindh desert to the lush pine trees and snow-capped peaks of Murree. I would pack my *bister* and watch as my mother sewed nametags onto every item of clothing, just as she had for my brothers. The fact that most children in my passport country did not experience this until 18 years old did not occur to any of us. This was normal life. We would never have thought to question it. What I didn't realize is that with this rite of passage, the comforts of home and shelter of unconditional love would end.

The best education for missionaries in Pakistan was Murree Christian School, situated in the beautiful foothills of the Himalayas. The school was a cooperative effort of several mission groups established in Pakistan, and it became a unique opportunity to put aside theological differences and focus on the shared need to educate the children of missionaries. The school made it possible for parents to stay in Pakistan with the assurance that their children would be prepared for higher education in their countries of citizenship.

I was seven when I joined my first Train Party. My imagination had gone wild with delight. What could be better than a party? I had dreamt of the day I would join other children heading off to school on this legendary and festive-sounding journey that marked the beginning and end of each school semester.

The day came, and I suddenly awoke from the dream. As we packed our luggage into the car, the reality hit me. This was goodbye. I was leaving home and leaving the security of home. I would no longer awaken in the security of my bedroom to the sight of my sleeping younger brother. Mom would no longer read me bedtime stories, or sing to me when I couldn't sleep.

I cried through the hour-long drive to the station. I cried because I had forgotten a doll at home, and I cried because I had just turned seven years old and 800 miles to home was as distant as the moon. I cried heavy sobs that racked my child body as I clutched my black stuffed lamb, sure that the world was coming to an end. At the station, eyes blinded by tears, I clung to Mom, crying in my heart, "Don't make me go. I can't leave you. You can't leave me!" The separation had happened too quickly. I was not ready.

Five minutes after the train pulled away, I was sitting with my friends, engaged in talk and play. I knew my mom had not died, I knew instinctively that I would see her again, but I also knew that her physical presence was no longer a reality in my world. So I did what most kids would do: I settled into my immediate surroundings, finding comfort where I could. I knew I had lost something, but I wasn't sure what it was. The loss was ambiguous. Mom was physically absent but present in my mind. I knew she would reappear ,but I had lost her all the same.

We arrived in Rawalpindi 18 hours later, our bodies grimy with dust, our food gone, and our journey almost complete. The bus ride up the mountain was bumpy and exciting. As difficult as it was to leave home, I was seeing friends who I had not seen for three months. A lot had happened in three months, and we talked and laughed, whispering secrets to each other, excited to be together once again. On arrival, house parents greeted us. We washed up and unpacked, claiming beds and dressers, trying to put our personal stamp onto institutional living.

For the next three months I shared a bedroom with seven roommates supervised by a housemother struggling to meet the needs of 20 to 30 little children, children who needed to eat, brush their teeth, bathe, dress, study, and sleep. Along with the practical needs were the emotional and spiritual needs. These were the unseen needs that satisfy the deepest of human longings; namely love and belonging.

It was a seemingly impossible task, but we would not know this until much later in our lives.

The first night I was exhausted and sleep came quickly. I woke disoriented, unsure of where I was. When I remembered, the blur and taste of hot, salty tears clouded my vision and lingered on my tongue. I dared not show my tears; it was not safe. We were all small, all facing separation and loss, all experiencing the first of many times of homesickness. We were surrounded by others as young as we were, by others with the same tears and fears, the same deep sense of loss. The scene would repeat itself each time I entered boarding school from the time I was six until the day I graduated. And each time, a cold, metal-framed bunk bed and the living God were my only witnesses. The one captured my tears, the other comforted them. With these two witnesses, I knew I could go on.

My memories of boarding school are happy and sad, much like anyone's childhood memories. Although separated from my parents so early, I knew that we were precious to them. It was more than intuition. My parents showed us that we were a priority. They surprised us with unexpected visits, listened to our school stories, and sent us letters and packages. And never in my memory did they utter the words, "We are sending you to boarding school so that we can do the work that God called us to." In the future, I would learn that other children were not so fortunate. I don't remember ever hearing the word "call." That word would enter my vocabulary later, and I would always have an uneasiness when hearing or using the word. But at the time, I never felt inferior to their work. I knew boarding school was about me, about my education and friends, not about giving Mom and Dad more time for the work that they did. I knew beyond doubt that if I ever needed my parents they would be on the next plane, train, or bus. They would move heaven and the

Pakistani transportation system so that they could be by my side. There was never a question as to their top priorities.

Nevertheless, after that first train party and each time I left on the train, as Mom's face grew more distant with each chug of the train's engine, I felt an acute loss. I strained my head as far out the window as I could for as long as I could until her face disappeared in a final cloud of dust, and I knew that home had been left behind. My early years of security and belonging had given way to constant movement and divided loyalties.

Murree Christian School, known to us as MCS, was housed in an old stone church built by the British to serve colonial officers and their families. The school took over the building in 1956, and gradually added additional classrooms, a dormitory with a large dining hall, kitchens, an infirmary, and studio apartments for house parents. The setting was idyllic. Murree was warm and green in the early summer, golden in the autumn months, white with snow on evergreens in the winter, and vivid with color and daisies in the springtime. Even the torrential rains and fog that swept in with the August monsoons were dramatically beautiful.

Our dormitory rooms varied in size and configuration with louvered windows along one end. I was often in a large room with four bunk beds. We shared dressers, drawers, and loft space, but our beds were our own. Each of us brought pieces of home – knick-knacks, a jewelry box, a family picture that would decorate our dressers. Our belongings were sparse, but we had plenty of space on the school grounds – a basketball court, monkey bars, and a front court that provided an excellent place for teenaged couples to sit, talking quietly, holding hands, and keeping each other's gaze until the bell rang, signaling the end of break. The *chai* shop across the street was a grungy, dilapidated building where *chai* poured from steaming kettles into tea glasses. This *chai* shop was off limits until we reached junior high school, but when we were finally allowed to cross the street and sit down at the worn tables, we would savor the hot sweet *chai*, warming us from the outside in. Along with this, we occasionally feasted on spicy omelets accompanied by delicious, *ghee*-filled *parathas*.

This school and its surroundings are etched on my memory. These were the places where my body grew and faith was formed. As I grew, these became my sacred places, places of beauty and belonging.

MURREE WAS IN close proximity to the disputed territory of Kashmir. From its beginnings, Pakistan's relationship with India was precarious, and Kashmir was the center of this conflict. We always seemed on the brink of war. Hence our evacuation suitcases. Each suitcase held clothing, water, and food with a shelf life of ten years or more. That meant Spam, beans, crackers, and tinned cheese.

The evacuation suitcases were meant for dire emergencies, but to a child they served a more immediate and practical function. As our normal supplies of special food from home dwindled, we raided the suitcases one by one, dividing up the Spam, the cheese, and the crackers. We left the beans. None of us cared much for those. But the other foods satisfied our growling tummies during evenings long after our house parents believed us to be asleep. Had we needed to escape through the mountains like the Von Trapps, we might not have survived for long. Fortunately – miraculously – we never needed the suitcases.

Emergency food was not all that disappeared. In preparation for our departure, Mom painstakingly and lovingly sewed little white tags bearing our names – Edward

Brown, Stanley Brown, Thomas Brown, Marilyn Brown, Daniel Brown – onto every shirt, sock, piece of underwear, and pair of pants. How Mom must have grieved as she sewed tiny stitches around the small white tags to ensure they would not come off during harsh washings in old-fashioned ringer washing machines. Despite the tags that marked them as ours, most of the socks and half of the underwear were missing at the end of three months.

Evacuation suitcases and nametags were among the rituals and symbols of our curious subculture. Other cultural markers included midnight feasts, Spring Sports Day, the Summer Carnival, tea time at four each afternoon, and study hall at seven each evening.

Midnight feasts were special times, organized by us, and sometimes, but not always, sanctioned by our house parents. We would gather food from wherever we could. Sometimes it was goodies from home, other times we bought sweets and savories in shops in the town of Murree, still other times we would beg the kitchen staff to sneak us cookies and homemade rolls. Stashing our food supplies under our beds, we excitedly set our alarms for midnight. At midnight, we would wake each other up and sneak to a pre-set location to eat, giggle, and talk. These feasts were amazing fixtures of our boarding school childhood. When we got older, the feasts sometimes included boys who walked a mile at midnight to sneak into our dorms. Nothing suspicious ever happened that I am aware of, but what teenager wouldn't want to be in a place where their crush would sneak into their lounge at midnight? Safety never entered the conversation, though it surely kept some of our house parents awake at night.

Spring sports days and summer carnivals were also part of our shared experience. Both were school-wide events with activities for every age level. Sports day divided the entire school into three teams: Red, Blue, and Yellow. We were divided according to the alphabet, and it was the luck of the draw as to which team had the most talent each year. I was on the Red Team, and our team usually lost. I like to think that we were all far more talented in the arts. The carnival was an equally exciting event and the whole school would come together to eat special food, participate in games, and make money for the Junior class.

Along with the events, homesickness and furloughs were part of the common vocabulary of our experience. We knew that our lives were significantly different from our peers in our home countries. But we only faced this directly every four or five years. When we did, isolation, loneliness, and a questioning of who we were shook our security and shaped our faith.

Our sub-culture also had its legendary figures. Auntie Doris was my house parent from age six to seven, and she might have walked out of an Enid Blyton boarding school story. Auntie Doris was mean. According to rumor, she was placed at the school because she lacked the language skills or psychological resilience to handle life in more remote areas of Pakistan. At MCS she could speak English, and interaction with Pakistanis was less demanding. But a call from God was a call from God. Who could dispute that? This was 1966, and missionaries did not feel the luxury to quibble about such things. So Auntie Doris was given charge of the most vulnerable of children, little girls.

Auntie Doris stories became wide-spread and terrifying. She inspected rooms with a white glove, meting out collective punishment when she found dust; she spanked little girls with a hairbrush enhanced with a nail; she forced a fourth grader to put her hand into an un-flushed toilet to retrieve candy wrappers. Whether the stories are true or false, they worked; most of us were terrified of Auntie Doris. She was a large, stern woman unequal to the task of caring for 24 little girls. After lights were out, only the most foolhardy of us would whisper to our roommates. Gathered for devotions in her room, we listened, for hours it seemed, as Auntie Doris read to us from a large Old Testament. We dared not yawn for fear of her wrath.

While I was under the care of Auntie Doris, my brother Stan broke his arm. It was late November of my first year in boarding. Autumn's golden leaves had fallen and cold had spread through the old stone buildings and dormitories. I remember fear spreading through me when I heard rumor, then the truth, then truth laced with rumor. Stan and his roommates had been playing superheroes, jumping off the top of their triple bunk beds onto a floor covered with mattresses. When he jumped, my brother's arm hit a space between two mattresses and badly fractured. The struggle of trying to make sense of this accident while in the care of an emotionally-absent houseparent was too much for me. I felt an agonizing confusion and acute emptiness. My brothers were my heroes. I didn't know what would happen to Stan. I desperately needed the reassurance of a parental figure to calm my fears and answer my questions. Would he be all right? Who would care for him? Would the arm heal? Oh, how I missed Mom.

A few days later she came. Mom was goodness and light and safety all wrapped into one. I understood Psalm 23 in a new way that moment. "*Yay! Though I walk through the valley of the shadow of death I will not fear, for Mama will be with me.*" I slept better that night than I had all semester. The message went soul-deep. If I needed my parents, they would be there. It didn't matter where I was, where they were, what had happened, whether I was at fault. They would come. They would walk me through the shadows. This assurance set down deep roots in my heart. I would know, eventually, that my God was like that too, and indeed that my parents were imitating Him.

I learned much later that after Mom left my room she went directly to the principal's house, in tears, to demand action on Auntie Doris. "It may be cold in Murree," she told him, "But it's icy in that little girls' dormitory!" Her concern was not with physical temperature; the frigid emotional climate made the physical cold seem balmy. Mom stayed just long enough to make everything better. She left Stan safe and comfortable with a cast on his fractured arm. She checked in with my brothers Ed and Tom and their respective house parents. And she did her best with Auntie Doris. More than all of this, she did something that erased guilt and left a deep spiritual mark.

A Danish evangelist spoke at school chapel while Mom was with us. He had come before, and each time he spoke his eloquence and passion rocked our chapel. He closed with the hymn, "Just as I am, without one plea / But that thy blood, was shed for me / And that thou bidst me come to thee / O Lamb of God I come, I come." By verse three, the weeping could be heard across the chapel. The child's prayer that I had prayed three years before in the city of Quetta was challenged each time the Danish evangelist came. At each altar call, I went forward. It didn't matter that the prayer uttered in Quetta was real, it didn't matter that I had already asked Jesus to forgive my sins and enter my little heart. What mattered was the deep sorrow I felt that I had grieved God and needed to repent and ask him into my heart again, and again, and again.

This time, because of my brother's broken arm, Mom was there. Once again my tears flowed. Once again I was about to go forward, to repent, to receive Jesus, again. Instead, I don't know how, I ended up sobbing in the arms of my mom. As I sobbed, she gently assured me that I didn't have to ask Jesus into my heart over and over and over again. Her gentle explanations and sound theology did their job; this was the end of my altar call journey. I never again went forward during a plea for repentance and salvation, and "Just as I Am" would never again manipulate me into doubting my salvation. I belonged to God, and to Mom, and no one could take that away.

Remarkably, my strongest memory of that year with Auntie Doris is a sweet memory. Midway through each semester, we had a school break for a "long weekend" of four or five days to allow most children to travel home to visit parents. Some of us lived too far away. Friends sometimes invited us to their homes, but this semester I was not so lucky. Along with three or four other girls, I was sentenced to spend the long weekend in boarding with Auntie Doris. To our astonishment, this long-weekend version of Auntie Doris was an altered Auntie Doris. She made us popcorn, took us for trips to town, read us special bedtime stories, and offered us delicious foods.

The biggest surprise of all came one bedtime. As I dozed off after a day of activity, snuggled in my bottom bunk with my stuffed lamb, I felt someone kneeling beside me. As I opened sleepy eyes, Auntie Doris reached over and kissed the top of my head. "Goodnight, Marilyn!" she whispered softly. Shock jolted me awake. Did it really happen? Auntie Doris, mean, terrible Auntie Doris, had kissed me!

Most of my memories of that year have faded. But that kiss from Auntie Doris, that contrast between what I had seen and experienced most of the year and what I experienced on one long weekend, showed me the complexity of human character. It also taught me the power of grace to shape and redeem memory. That bedtime kiss is my most durable memory of a year that might have left permanent scars. This would be a repeated theme of my boarding school experience. Poignant hard times and overwhelming happy times made their mark with indelible ink on the story of my life, and my faith was shaped, not shattered, by these memories. Through those years, and many that followed, I have come to know God as the "Memory Keeper."

At the end of my first year an angel arrived. She was tall and pretty, she had a God-given love for "her little girls," and her voice confirmed her celestial credentials. Auntie Eunice came to Pakistan on a college internship, and she fell in love. But the object of her devotion was not a man; it was the students at Murree Christian School. When she returned to Canada at the end of her internship, she evidently said to God that if she could work with kids at Murree the rest of her life, she would not care about marriage or a family. God granted this request, and she entered into life at MCS as the little girls' housemother. Auntie Eunice read us stories, curled our hair, and made us fudge. She welcomed us to her small studio apartment, which she decorated with color and flair. She dressed with the same flair. She was beautiful, she was smart, she sang, and she listened. The contrast with Auntie Doris was startling, and wonderful. Wounds slowly healed and we happily settled into this new normal.

In the spring of second grade, I suffered a new wound that would leave an enduring scar. I was often ill in those first years in boarding school. One day I was kept after school. Everyone knew I was faking, my teacher told me. I was to stop it. Just stop. Who was "everyone"? I didn't know, but I was quite sure that all of the boarding and teaching staff were talking about me. The words hit me the way they were intended. I would not be sick again. I felt completely misunderstood. I remember walking slowly out of the classroom, my face burning with shame. What would I tell my friends? The only secrets we had were those that were cried into our pillows at night. Would I cry this secret into my pillow, or would I share it?

My friends were waiting. "What happened?" Five little girls crowded around me at our afternoon tea-time. "She thinks I'm faking." There. I had put my shame into words. Maybe it wouldn't have so much power over me. But it did. I was not sick again during that semester. But the damage was severe, and it multiplied in strength; each time the memory awoke, I cringed with embarrassment and accusation. I internalized the accusation, and secretly branded myself an impostor, a scarlet letter emblazoned on my heart.

In June, at the close of the spring semester, Mom arrived to collect me. I learned much later that a houseparent pulled mom aside to tell her of the concern that I was fabricating illness and the staff didn't quite know what to do with me. Mom was beside herself with worry and fear. Did she have a daughter who was so damaged that she was feigning illness? Dad was still far away in Sindh, unreachable by telephone, and she was single parenting five children who ranged from a preschooler to a teenager. With nowhere else to turn, she approached a doctor and close family friend who was working in the summer missionary clinic.

Dr. John Bavington lived with his wife Mary and their children in the city of Peshawar where he practiced both physical medicine and psychiatry. He was a unique practitioner in a country where care for diseases of the mind was rare. As John checked me over, he puzzled over my symptoms, finally concluding, "I think she has amoeba. Let's get stool samples and try to isolate the parasites." It took him a long time to identify the amoeba, invisible rascals that these parasites are, but he finally isolated them and put me on a course of treatment. Mom's relief was intense. Her child was not damaged, and she was vindicated.

Sometimes the parts of the story we don't remember are the most important. I did not remember the chapter of the story in which I was the victim of a parasite that was feeding off my body. I only recalled the chapter in which I was told to stop faking. I remembered the version in which I stood, face down, burning with the heat of shame. I remembered the version in which I wanted to cry foul and explain myself, the part where I felt misunderstood and alone. I only remembered the accusation, not the vindication.

During the summer, I ate fresh vegetables and fruits and rested at home. When fall came, I went into boarding again. I would not be sick again for a significant amount of time, until my sixth grade year, when I learned how to put the thermometer just close enough to a light bulb to watch it rise to a perfect low-grade fever of 99.4 degrees. Anything more might have been suspect, but 99.4 guaranteed that I would be left in the dorm while classmates went on to school, giving me the opportunity to be by myself and get some much needed time alone. Ironically, I was never caught, nor was I ever again accused of faking illness.

IN THE SPRING of third grade, Lizzy Hover's dad died. A year younger than me and the third of four children, Lizzy was curly-haired and vibrant. She was full of personality, with a sense of humor that resonated with mine. I loved Lizzy. She was fun and honest, and even as a young girl she didn't care what people thought of her. One year, Lizzy wrote a book report on a book that she had made up. Unfortunately, she wrote it so poorly that the teacher asked her to go fetch the book from the library in order to help her improve on the assignment. Unlike the rest of us, Lizzy was able to emerge from this unscathed. That was Lizzy Hover.

I heard Lizzy sobbing early one Sunday morning, and my heart filled with dread. Lizzy Hover didn't cry. As my roommates and I waited silently in our beds, we knew something was terribly wrong. From my top bunk with a clear view out the door, I saw Lizzy walking down the hall with Auntie Eunice, and I was filled with fear. A short while later Auntie Eunice gathered us together in her apartment to relay the tragic news. The school had received a telegram. Peter Hover, Lizzy's father and a beloved British doctor, had died in a road accident.

Peter and his wife Carol, also a doctor, served in the Caravan Christian Hospital. They transported an entire mobile hospital to remote areas of the Sindh region to offer health care clinics and surgeries to people without any access to medical care. When the accident happened, the Hovers were heading to Murree, where their three older children, David, Meg and Lizzy, were in boarding school. Their youngest child, Janet, was with them. Peter and Carol were each driving a different vehicle, when a sudden storm of dust, created by busses, surrounded their vehicles. Peter's vehicle collided head-on with an oncoming bus.

My parents, miles away in Hyderabad, were among the first to learn of the accident. In *Jars of Clay*, Mom recalled those days so long ago:

> *In the searing heat of the day, not a breath of breeze blew across the landscape. Whenever a car passed or went off onto the shoulder, a cloud of dust hung in the still air, blocking visibility. About 200 miles north of Hyderabad, Carol realized she could no longer see Peter behind her. Several new buses, traveling south together to Karachi*

*had passed them throwing up that monstrous cloud of
dust. Stopping at the edge of the narrow highway, she
saw people running toward the road. "There must have
been an accident," she said, "and Peter has stopped to help."
But Peter would not be helping. He had been seriously
injured. Perhaps he had lost his bearings in the cloud of
dust; perhaps the bus that hit him head on had strayed to
the wrong side of the road. Peter Hover died there beside
the highway, his badly injured head cradled in his wife's
arms.....*

Pauline A Brown, *Jars of Clay*

Carol, Janet, and a young nurse Cecelia arrived to their
home in Hyderabad with Peter's body. It was after midnight,
and there was no undertaker to call, no funeral home to help
with arrangements. Dad and Dr. Carol bathed the body and
prepared it for burial. They then laid him in our guest room
surrounded by ice, a ceiling fan blowing air from high above.

Peter Hover's death had a huge impact on my parents,
and on me. The Hovers were dear friends, around my mom
and dad's age, and fellow workers in Sindh. We saw the Hover
family frequently. The loss was acute. We all knew the Hover
children, and we all knew their parents. We were a small
community and our tragedies were shared. So we grieved
for Lizzy, Meg, and David. And we grieved for ourselves.
If it could happen to their father, what would stop it from
happening to my father? None of us were safe. This was the
first time I had experienced death. Each time I experienced
another tragedy, the memory resurfaced and reopened the
wound of Peter Hover's death.

After a leave in the UK, Carol Hover returned to Pakistan
with her children, where she began practicing as a physician
at Shikarpur Christian Hospital, the women's and children's

hospital set up by my parents' mission. The hospital had been at a crisis point, and my parent's mission was wondering if it could stay open. Doctors and nurses were tired and more staff were desperately needed. The untimely death of Peter Hover was a tragedy; that Dr. Carol would not hesitate to return to Pakistan and use her skills as a physician in Shikarpur was a gift to hundreds of people and one of the great mysteries of life. Cynics might call this mystery a cruel turn of fate, while believers see it as God's grace despite the tragedy of a broken world. I grew up with people that believed it was the latter.

In the following years, while on school vacations, I would often see Carol Hover by the bedside of a patient, praying. When we visited Shikarpur, I would run through the hospital corridors with Meg and Lizzy, briefly forgetful of the tragedy.

One winter visit when I was twelve, when the Hover family was living in a ward of the hospital, Meg introduced me to Ian Fleming's James Bond novels. I was frightened, and excited, by their raciness. But James Bond still faced stiff competition for my attention from Enid Blyton's boarding school stories. After small doses of the adult world, we tired of it, always returning to the familiar and relatable. I read and pretended for hours with the Hover kids in a small room that would later serve as a medication room after the hospital became fully functional.

Carol Hover became one of many women who modeled life for me. She had strength and fortitude. She knew grace. She wore character, humor, and dignity along with her white doctor's coat and stethoscope. As a girl I watched her and would silently marvel. It was like watching a stage-play in which the actors face extraordinary challenges but refuse to abandon the script or walk off stage. Was this faith? I was beginning to see it as such.

Tragedies were a background to our lives. We saw deformities and disability; illness claimed the lives of babies, children, and adults; tragic accidents were common. I don't remember feeling squeamish or morbid about this. Perhaps early on we learned that life could be extinguished in the briefest second. The words in Urdu, *Insha'Allah,* if God wills, were part of our vocabulary, spoken by Muslims, echoed by Christians. God was author of life. God was author of death. There seemed little any of us could do; we were participants in the story, not its author.

Because we were not shielded from these tragedies, early on I would create in my mind an album of the unexplainable. This album began with Peter Hover's death, and it has filled through the years. A permanent fixture in my mind, it will never be lost or left behind. I knew early on that some things would never, ever make sense. So my album began with Lizzy Hover's early-morning tears and the news of her father's death.

Peter Hover died in the spring, and that summer our family left for a year-long furlough. We moved to Fitchburg, Massachusetts, to Klondike Avenue, just a short distance from Highland Baptist, my parents' home church. If there was any time when our lives reflected the normal experience of other American children, this was it.

Klondike Avenue was perfect. We rented a New England home perched on an incline with a large lawn stretching down to the street. I loved this house with its den, patio, and large eat-in kitchen. There were four bedrooms and a large, finished attic that functioned as a game room. There was always a Risk game spread out on the floor, my older brothers competing to conquer the world. Best of all, the house came with instant friendships. We rented from Rodney and Lucy Pierce, members of Highland Baptist, and several members of the extended Pierce family lived on our street and opened their homes and their hearts to us. The Russ Pierces had a pool where we swam on summer afternoons; the Rodney Pierces had a huge back field, perfect for softball on spring evenings; and each week I walked to the A-frame at the end of the street for piano lessons with Sandy Waaramaa. Carin Waaramaa, Sandy's daughter, came to our door the day we moved in to introduce herself in a shaky voice. We became best friends, and I can't imagine what 4th grade would have been without Carin.

Into a world that I did not understand, the Waaramaa family brought not just piano lessons, but security and love. A few years ago when I heard the news of Carin's death, my heart hurt. She died young, leaving behind a son in elementary school and a young daughter. Carin's death severed a fragile bond to a memorable year in my life.

Our "normal" year flew by. We enrolled in day school, where we drank white milk from small cardboard cartons. We attended church and Sunday school. I went to Pioneer girls; my brothers attended youth group. We did what Christian American families did, and we did it well. But when the year ended, we were not reluctant to leave. Pakistan beckoned us. Throughout the year, friends had written to us on aerogrammes, keeping us apprised of life back home. In Fitchburg we were novelties, our status elevated in our 'missionary' role, and the novelty could only be sustained for so long. In fact, it was already growing thin. It was time to get back to the places and people where we kids were most comfortable.

But this time we would be leaving my brother Ed behind, returning to Pakistan as a family of six rather than seven. I was ten years old, as egocentric as is possible. Yet even I wondered how we were going to do this. How could we break apart this family of ours? But I was incapable of imagining how wrenching this decision was for my parents and my brother. They had talked it out together. Ed would stay with Uncle Jim and Aunt Jean in Winchendon. He would finish high school at Murdock High School. Ed was mature. He had mastered the role of oldest child. But he would never be a full part of our family in the same way. He would grow up quickly, faced with a pregnant classmate, drug-using peers, and a struggling youth group. I would be back in Pakistan, hearing only sound bites, and living with all the egocentric gusto of youth at the brink of puberty. It was three years before I saw Ed again. When I did, he was engaged to be married. While I was still a child, he became a man.

A year later, I sat beside Mom at what would have been my brother's high school graduation. Insensitive to the grief she was experiencing, I was petulant and self-centered, impatient to leave the auditorium for punch and cake, while Mom, through her tears, frantically wrote notes to the graduates. These were Ed's classmates. This was his time. He should have been there celebrating, with his classmates and my parents, this milestone in his life. Instead, he was oceans away in a small town in New England. This was the cost of a life overseas. Mom had committed to this life, having no idea what would be required. She was living out the requirements, the sacrifice, in front of me and I had no idea.

Years before, when Ed was six years old, he had nearly drowned in the waters of a canal. At that time, Mom had been struggling with the idea of sending a child to boarding school. The pain of sending such a young child away seemed like far too much to ask of her. Then on a warm day soon before Ed turned six, Mom went on a picnic with our friends, the Addletons, to a canal nearby. Dad was traveling, and Mom was watching over Stan, and Tom, both active toddlers. Ed played happily with a toy boat near the canal. Mom turned her head away, and when she looked back Ed was nowhere to be seen. Quickly they realized that he had fallen into the canal. Hu Addleton dove into the canal, but came up twice empty handed. The third time, he brought up the lifeless, muddy body of my brother. Pulling mud and debris from my brother's mouth, Mom began to pray. She started chest compressions and basic CPR. Miraculously, my brother lived.

Something changed in Mom the day that Ed was rescued. The miracle was so profound that it became the hallmark of God's care for her children. I was not even a thought in my parents' mind at the time, but I grew up with this family story. It was our own family miracle. The night of graduation I believe might have been almost as difficult as the day that she thought she had lost him. As the auditorium emptied of people, Mom did the same thing she had done twelve years earlier – she gave my brother to God. But I was oblivious as I sat beside her, blind to the emotions that stirred in her.

FOR THE THREE months a year that the whole family lived in Murree we lived two distinct lives, home life and boarding school life. The one common link was school; everything else was different. Home life was rustic. During monsoon rains our floors were dotted with buckets and pans to catch the leaks, and the walls and floors were perpetually damp and dingy. Our toilet was a wooden commode with a portable tin pot that had to be emptied twice a day. We were a short step up from camping. Year to year we moved from house to house. We rented from Presbyterians, Methodists, or Evangelical Alliance missionaries, and all the houses had names: Park House, Rosenheim, Kuldana Cottage, Forest Dell. A romantic may have called them cottages, but the reality was quite different. They were small, and squeezing in a family of seven was a challenge. Mom hung thin curtains across a rope to offer some privacy to whichever family member was entering puberty at the time. As the only girl, I gloried in having a room of my own from the time I was ten years old through the remainder of my time at home. Though we never owned these houses, their walls held the memories and the secrets of our childhood and adolescence.

In Murree, Mom moved and dressed with greater freedom. Women could wear western-style clothes and walk freely on the hillside paths. She worked hard to create a sense of home. Despite meager household supplies, we enjoyed delicious homemade meals, fresh-baked bread, and we often arrived home to large bowls of fresh plums and apricots. During the school day, Mom made jams to last through the year, pickles to enjoy with our sandwiches, and kept up with the massive chore of feeding and caring for a large family with no short cuts and no ready-made foods. This could not have been easy, and it was another display of Mom's resilience. She walked miles to get together with the moms of my friends, taught Sunday School, and struggled to offer stability to her five children. Mom would later write that this was the time of the year that felt most familiar, most 'normal' to her.

Coming home from school daily instead of heading back to a dormitory room was a welcome change. We entered the front door to the smell of homemade brownies and to the sight of large bowls of fruit on the table. Mom worked to give us a healthier diet than we were accustomed to at the school. We took homemade lunches to school daily, bringing extra treats for less fortunate schoolmates whose parents were unable to come to Murree during the summer.

During these summers, Mom participated in our lives in the ways she always wanted to. She waited to greet us after school, to ask about our day. We talked, did homework, ate dinner together, and functioned as a family. This was the kind of parenting that had been modeled for her in her own childhood. But it was only for a few months during the summer. My father did not have even this luxury. He was alone in the heat of Sindh with no air conditioner and the expectation that he would continue functioning in the work of the mission. Mom and Dad missed each other tremendously during these times, particularly in the years where some of their children tried their patience through experimentation with anything that wasn't allowed.

On summer Sunday nights we walked along the Mall in the town of Murree to services at Holy Trinity Church. For me the attraction was social, never spiritual. My friends were often there, and as we grew older, we pleaded with our parents to allow us to sit together. We would sit as far back in the church as possible, tiptoeing out, two-by-two, to buy soft-serve ice cream from a nearby shop. During closing hymns, we tiptoed back, imagining the adults in our lives to be none the wiser. I loved those times, and I remember them with little guilt and a great deal of pleasure.

IN THE SUMMER of first grade I began a life-long love affair with Julie Andrews and *The Sound of Music*. A diplomat from the Canadian Embassy in Islamabad was able to obtain the film, and the school administration granted permission to show it to the entire school during school hours. To the "innocent minds" of Murree Christian School, this was a momentous event. For a school that catered to a wide spectrum of beliefs and wide variations in tolerance for what was and wasn't appropriate for kids – my dad hated playing cards, another father disapproved of any physical touch between couples – showing a "mainstream" movie like *The Sound of Music* was risky. Evidently, those in high power previewed the film and deemed it suitable for the young minds of missionary children – ages six to 18. The school actually cancelled classes so that the entire student body could watch it.

The day of the movie we left Park House for school as usual. By the end of the day, I was changed forever. The first note of "The Hills are Alive" captured me. I became Maria – Maria of the dirndl and guitar, singing with confident joy on her beautiful hills, Maria the young nun misunderstood by the others, Maria the young beauty in love with the Austrian naval officer. But my six-year-old self was not just enraptured by the beautiful music and dramatic retelling of the Von Trapp family story. In the midst of all the singing, the beauty, the love story, I saw that men had the ability to make choices: choices that were good and choices that were evil. It was the precursor to what I would learn later: in the midst of all that was lovely and beautiful in Murree, all that I loved, there was dysfunction, there was bad, sometimes there was evil.

In movies, I could handle the paradox of good and evil; good always triumphed. But as I grew in both body and faith in our real world, good did not always triumph. There would always be an album of the unexplainable. In Murree, as we travelled the seasons from fresh air and spring daisies, to crisp fall apples and the smell of wood fires in late October, we grew older and gradually lost innocence, sometimes through our own actions and sometimes through the actions of others. The *Sound of Music* captured the innocence of my childhood even as it introduced me to a more complex world.

AMONG THE MANY lovely things that Murree had to offer, perhaps the finest was the perfect afternoon tea. Tea had been a part of my life since I graduated from mother's milk. Whether English tea or Pakistani *chai*, tea soothed and calmed, brought perspective and healing, and turned bad days into good. *High tea* took all the best in tea and added a dose of elegance. And the most delightful place for high tea was Lintotts on the Mall in Murree. Lintotts was a little girl's dream. Its wide veranda overlooked the Mall, a vestige of days when sipping afternoon tea on a veranda was a primary occupation of British army wives.

Tea service at Lintotts was an art. Tiny china pots of strong tea were complemented by little pitchers of warm milk and sugar bowls covered with bead-edged netting to guard against flies. Three-tiered floral china plates were filled with pastries, some chocolate, some vanilla, and all creamy. Lintotts elderly, turbaned waiters were attentive to every need, and would surely have drawn Jane Austen's attention, had she ever been fortunate enough to have tea at Lintotts. In fact, this was a high tea that would have fit perfectly into Jane Austen's world of light humor and delightful, entertaining company who were never morose or depressing.

Lintotts was a special outing for Mom and me. My brothers were never part of it. I don't remember much conversation. Talk was unnecessary. Just being there, being together, was the delight. High tea transported me into a make-believe grown-up world. Problems, worries, and frustrations faded in the quiet noise of spoons against china cups and muted conversation. Then, finally, after the last sip of tea, and after the last clink of silver spoons on china cups, we began the long walk home, up and down the hills of Murree, rested and sure of one thing: life needed times reserved for tea, uninterrupted and fully at peace. I have never forgotten that lesson.

There was a darker side to high tea I would only confront much later. This pleasure that so delighted me as a little girl was a survival of Pakistan's colonial past. The "British Raj" era, or the era of British rule, lasted for almost 100 years. It included the entire Indian subcontinent. Pakistan was born in 1948, and my parents arrived only five years later. I was completely blind to my privilege as a little, white, English-speaking girl. I cringe now at what I took for granted. Those who were white and English-speaking went to the head of the line. Those who were white and English-speaking could casually criticize Pakistanis without thought. We traveled where we pleased, we went first class or third class on trains – it was our choice. We were educated and would have a world of opportunity. I thank God for parents that had the conscience and determination to discipline me and teach me in various ways that I was not better than those around me. Still, with a strong personality and ego to match, those lessons sometimes fell on ears unwilling to listen and a heart that would need continual reminders that privilege is not something I earned or deserved.

My MEMORIES OF boarding are kept alive through an album of letters, written in a child's uneven script and carefully preserved by my mother. The letters span my childhood from age six to 18. The early letters are brief, in neat penmanship.

Many years have passed since I painstakingly composed letters into words, words into sentences, and sentences into paragraphs, finally handing the letter to a hawk-eyed teacher who would judge it worthy to be sent to parents. Parents,

I might add, who missed us so much that they could not possibly have cared about penmanship or grammar. The irony is profound.

My earliest letters reflect a deep, sisterly concern for my youngest brother, Danny, still at home with my parents. With run-on sentences and widely divergent thoughts I ask about a sweater my mother was knitting, thank my parents for a family picture, and end the letter with greetings and love for Danny and Daddy. I talk about trying to help house parents and not being homesick because "I get to come home soon." Every letter begins with the date on the left corner, a greeting of "Dear Family" and a sentence or two specifically about Danny, the importance of Danny. I was zealous for his welfare: *How is Danny? Is Danny lonesome? Does Danny miss me? Is Danny having fun with the kitty? Say 'hi' to Danny. I miss Danny.* In later letters my concern for siblings extends to my older brothers: *Eddy is sick. Stanley bought me peanut butter. Tommy asked Nancy Kennedy to the banquet. Don't tell him that I told you.*

I was slightly in awe of Ed. He was seven years older than me, teased me least, and I adored him. I talked about him for hours to my friends after he left home. Stanley was the life of our family with a quick wit and a fast tongue. I was most like him. Both of us could raise our parents' wrath more quickly than our siblings could. We did not fear conflict; we often looked for it. Tom was the brilliant middle child. It wasn't until I was in the U.S. for my first year of high school that I learned how cute he was. I became popular to girls who imagined I was the doorway to his heart. How wrong they were.

It was Tom who tutored me so that I would pass my Physics final in junior year; Tom who helped to push me up a mountain when I was ready to give up; and Tom who would phone me during my college years to make sure I was eating right. I was sitting in our school infirmary when I heard news that Tom had broken his leg. I remember looking at the messenger and wanting to kill them. They spoke with such confidence that he would be okay. *How did they know?* I thought with anger. He was *my* brother. They weren't related to him. I cared about Tom far more than they did. Soon after, I ran to my dorm room and threw myself on my bed, bursting into tears. Alone on my bed, I sobbed and I sobbed. In the meantime, Tom was being rushed to a hospital to have his leg put into a cast. I would not see him until later, when he was surrounded by sympathetic friends and had become a hero of sorts. I watched shyly from the sidelines, a sibling who felt like a stranger. My heart was still hurting but his presence confirmed that the messengers had been right – he was okay.

Danny, my youngest brother, was wise beyond his years. One of the first pictures of the two of us shows me on tiptoe, scowling over his crib. I must have instinctively known that this little baby was competition for Mom and Dad's attention, and I would have none of it. But then, in a completely uncharacteristic act of kindness, I gave him a doll.

After my older brothers were launched from the family nest, and only Dan and I were left at boarding school, I began to appreciate him more, and deeply wanted his admiration. He had mine because of his intelligence and wisdom; I needed his as well.

Sibling relationships are strange. We grow up together, eat at the same dinner table, are loved and nurtured, disciplined and scolded by the same parents. We sit together around Christmas trees or *Eid* feasts, go together to churches, mosques, or synagogues. Our siblings have similar features, characteristics, and memories. But sibling relationships are complex and perplexing. Boarding school undoubtedly adds another layer to that complexity. Should I acknowledge siblings when at boarding school? Some of us did, some didn't. Should I look to them for guidance and comfort? Or will I allow them to grow distant even as I see them every day, like the faces of my parents at the train station?

The distance that grows between many siblings as they grow older threatened to separate us early, before we were ready. Older siblings became teenagers, and peer pressure and other concerns diverted their interest from younger brothers and sisters. We who were younger were left wondering what had happened. When did the ease with which we had communicated, laughed, and fought turn into difficulty trying to figure out what to say to each other? When did a solid relationship turn sketchy and strained? When did I become an embarrassment to my older brothers? Was it when I gained weight? Was it when I was punished, and gossip spread through school's well-oiled rumor mill?

The embarrassment ended, though I don't know when. Blood runs thick in our family, and ties are strong, carrying with them an innate recognition of the importance of being siblings. In life's journey, we knew that siblings mattered; sometimes they were all we had.

IN THIRD GRADE our class staged a play on the theme of gossip. Esmeralda, the lead character, was a little girl, like us, in boarding school. We all memorized the theme song. "*Gossip, gossip, gossip, evil a thing,*" we sang in unison. "*Much unhappiness it brings,*" we continued, completely ignoring the warning, and the advice that followed: "*If you can't say something nice, Don't talk at all is my advice.*"

We lived in close quarters, usually six or eight to a room. Bunk beds lined the walls. We shared dresser space, bathroom space, three-inch baths twice a week, and secrets.

We had best friends and bitter enemies. We knew what it was to be mean, and for others to be mean to us. Survival as a six-year-old in boarding school depended on savvy and on learning to negotiate the social challenges of a six-year-old world. Survival was sometimes about gossiping or listening to gossip. Survival was also about sharing, crying, fighting, and hiding our indescribable homesickness. The odd thing is that most of us wouldn't trade it. Boarding school was like life – a paradox. We would just learn that lesson earlier than most of our peers in our passport countries.

As we grew older, gossip became more insidious, more destructive. Our school was small. Everyone knew everyone's business. I would grow to deeply miss this tight community after I left, but while I was there, I suffered, as did others, from secret telling and sharing, from meanness and gossip. When I became the subject of gossip, life was intolerable. But I still had to go on. I ate, studied, slept, and played with the same people. There was nowhere to escape. I had to bear the discomfort until the winds changed, and another person was the victim. It's what we did. We survived. This survival was just life. I never thought about it. I did what I had to. I tried to please those who were popular. I was mean to those who weren't. And I had my soul-friends that I could trust, who bring a smile to my face as I remember them.

We didn't put spiritual language on gossip, although our house parents did. But the fact that it occurred within an insular community and Christian context made it worse, and I still hate gossip even as I am still drawn into it like a small child in boarding school.

OUR LARGE AUDITORIUM was the center of the school building. It also functioned as our main meeting place. All of the classrooms were located off the auditorium, and so at break, lunch times, or the end of the day, we would spill out into the auditorium, a sea of children from twelve through eighteen. Every day around noon the mail arrived. Mail delivery was a highlight of our day. In elementary school, our house parents collected the mail and called our names one by one. In junior high and high school, we gathered at the school office where mail was sorted into little boxes.

We would exit our classrooms quickly and head toward the area at the front of the building where the main office and the principal's office were located. Whether it was a plain envelope or a blue aerogramme, mail was exciting. It signified connections with the world outside, connection with parents, with friends who had left Pakistan, with relatives from the United Kingdom or the United States, Sweden or Germany.

Three times a term Mom and Dad sent packages, always shoebox size, wrapped in brown paper and tied with string, sometimes sealed with wax. I rushed to find a private space amidst a crowd to open this treasure. I knew even before I opened the package what it would hold: 8 brownies, separated into two layers; thick, tangy, lemon squares wrapped in wax paper, reinforced with thick aluminum foil; homemade cookies; and fudge. Often mom sent a small jar containing homemade jelly or marshmallow fluff carefully wrapped in paper to keep the glass from shattering on the long, bumpy ride from the Sindh desert to our school's pine-forested mountains. Mom always included a note.

As much as I wanted to keep the package to myself, at least for a few minutes, the unspoken rules were clear. The popular kids took a share. Of course, I shared with Nancy, my best friend. And then, well, some kids never got packages from home and empathy demanded that I give them a bite or two.

And before I knew it, the package was gone, disappearing as quickly as Mom's face through the train window or as Dad's voice echoing from the train platform.

Those brown paper packages were a reminder that I was special, tangible proof that I had parents, and that from 800 miles away they cared about me. Though I sometimes felt lost in boarding school, at home I had parents who prayed for me, thought of me, baked for me.

Packages told an unwritten story of a mom who baked in the heat to make sure she had our favorite goodies to send. A mom who laid everything out on the table, wrapping, and packing, making sure that all was equally distributed. Packages told of a dad who went about his daily work with a stop at the post office, chatting with the postman about politics, the weather, and the price of onions. A dad who made sure that these well-wrapped treasures made it via an inefficient postal system from the desert of Sindh to the green mountains of Murree. Packages were concrete proof of family and home, of belonging and love.

My world of packages and boarding school is long gone. The packages I now receive are generally from a bookseller, delivering books to our apartment, the packages lying on the ground until someone gets home to dust them off and take them inside. But recently there was a package, wrapped carefully, first in a white envelope, then in brown paper. It was a gift from someone I had never met. My heart leapt, just like it used to when I was a little girl opening up that package with brownies and lemon squares. Some things never grow old — and "brown paper packages tied up with string" must be one of them.

Nothing is simple, and when it comes to boarding school and attitudes to boarding school, I learned early on to be capable of complexity. Just as packages, for all their delight, came with their challenges, so it is with boarding school. Even now when people find out that I went to boarding school, they pause. They don't know how to begin the conversation, but eventually it comes out. The conversation is awkward and at some point, they have to spit it out: "How did your mom do that? That must have been so hard!"

It's always a matter-of-fact statement, and I deeply appreciate that the person is trying to communicate, to move into my world, to understand it. But nothing is ever that simple. Yes, it was hard. My experience certainly included bone-chilling sadness and unstoppable aches. And it was also wonderful. It was full of stomach-aching laughter and tears of joy.

Many of us find it hard to reconcile the good with the bad. For years, I thought it would be disloyal to my parents if I talked about the hard. I have come to realize that most of the things that I found hard, they too found difficult. Reducing boarding school to a single experience or story fails to do it justice. It's far more complex than a single story.

Boarding school – like the life of any child – was paradoxical. It was marked by tears at train stations, goodbyes that left a pit in my stomach, early morning wake up on the first day of boarding, confused and disoriented, and the evil of gossip. Boarding was homesickness and misunderstanding, wishing Mom would be there, only to feel unable to communicate once she arrived. Boarding school with its rules and institutional living wasn't easy. From bunk beds to dressers, all of our living space was shared. We bathed once a week in three inches of water, and washed our hair once a week unless we melted snow. Boarding school separated us from our families, even when we saw our siblings. We learned to relate to family in a completely new way. We had to learn crowd control and learn who could make our lives miserable, or comfortable. It was community living – at its worst, but also at its best.

We made life-long friends and relished deep conversation. We experienced the excitement of train parties and sipped hot chai at train stations. We loved story time at night, performing plays after school, midnight feasts, and picnics at a large rock we called Big Rock located in the woods that surrounded our hostel. We played Kick the Can and Flashlight Beckon until we were called in for bed. We shared secrets and friendship, boyfriends and deep discussions. We went on camping trips, drank late-night chai around rickety tables with friends, held hands with boys on Sunday night walks, and sang for hours to an old guitar. We discovered who we were and struggled to understand what we believed in conversations that I remember to this day.

For many moms, sending a child to boarding school is probably a bit like giving them up for adoption. You are entrusting another to care for that child whom you birthed, whom you love, who holds your heart. Your heart has to expand and let others speak into your child's daily life. My parents faced criticism from well-meaning folks, and when we visited the United States Mom often had to bite her tongue in the face of self-righteous comments and barely veiled criticism: "You may be able to send your kids to boarding school, but I could never do that."

I knew beyond doubt that Mom and Dad loved me. They understood that they were never the primary authors of their children's story. That authorship belonged to God, and they were the writing instruments. So they wrote on our lives and allowed others to write as well. Some of my boarding parents wrote words of wisdom, laughter, joy, and discipline. Others weren't sure what to write. And some, in their human frailty, wrote carelessly or cruelly.

Auntie Eunice wrote music and joy into my childhood world. From the time I met her at age seven, her angelic voice rang through the halls of our dormitory. I always knew when she was coming. Sometimes I would say I was homesick just so I could have Auntie Eunice to myself. She mothered us well, yet always gave us up without a grudge when our real moms came to reclaim us. We were always her kids.

Deb wrote chapters into my life when I was a teenager, when boys and belief were complicated and I was learning to work out my faith with fear and trembling. Deb's small studio apartment had room for my cooking, my laughter, and my tears – sometimes falling so fast it was hard to keep up. Deb loved me when I was unlovable and kept in touch with me when I faced the daunting task of returning to my passport country for college. She was more friend than housemother.

Deb and Eunice taught me to love well, without holding too tight. They taught me about sacrifice and perseverance. They taught me about laughter and the long journey. As I grew, they became my friends – friends I could pray with, cry with, and laugh with until the wee morning hours.

But the unseen woman in the story is Mom, offstage but always instrumental. She gave me to God and prayed for those who could walk beside me when she wasn't there. It could have easily gone another way. I know adults whose boarding school journey was so painful that it is a closed chapter in their lives. I know others who are bitter and desperately look for answers and healing. This could easily have been me. I have learned to trust God as the memory keeper, and recognize that there was grace in the space between.

Boarding school brought with it joys and losses that cannot be dissected until later in life. Boarding school was the good and the terrible, the happy and the sad, the laughter and the tears. I learned that grace covers memories, and magic can happen in unlikely places; that one bad houseparent doesn't define your life; and that forgiveness is a necessary ingredient of life. Boarding school crammed most of life's lessons into twelve years.

STAGED EACH YEAR before the winter holidays, the Christmas pageant was symbolic of the end of term and our return home. We loved acting, and we frequently staged shows in our lounge, even without an audience. The pageant offered a larger stage and an audience of adults. We sometimes performed at the annual dinner that was designed to show appreciation to the national staff at the school. It was an important event, a time to show gratitude to the Pakistanis who worked tirelessly and often quite anonymously. As self-centered children, caught up in our own games, we often forgot their names.

I was never Mary; always a wiseman, never a Mary. I desperately wanted to be Mary, with her blue robe and glowing perfection. But I had a short, pixie haircut and I was on the stocky side. Stocky, short-haired Mary wouldn't do. The honor went instead to my pretty best friend, Nancy. With olive skin, long dark hair, and deep brown eyes, Nancy was a natural for Mary.

But my desire never changed. I knew that some parts are better than others. Like the Sunday School teacher in *The Best Christmas Pageant Ever*, teachers may say over and over that there are no small parts, just small actors and that every part is just as important as every other part. But kids are smarter than that. We knew that Mary was the most important. And we also knew that the part required long, beautiful black hair and dark eyes, not a short pixie cut and a stocky body. That for sure would move you into the lesser role of shepherd or wiseman. But as long as there was a pageant, I wanted to be Mary. Disguised as a wiseman in purple robe, bearing beautiful brass from the bazaar, internally I was Mary.

At Murree, there were other 'Mary' parts – solos at school concerts, awards at ceremonies, prizes for Scripture memorization or perfect attendance. As a child I longed for those parts, longed to be Mary, but in the elementary years, I found myself playing the wiseman, come from afar. I looked on in envy, and only slowly grew to value the role of the wiseman. Contentment is a process that can come and go, depending on our willingness to accept the roles that life brings. Boarding school both helps and hurts that process – it helps because in many ways we were forced to grow up quickly. In other ways, we learned to fight inside what we saw as unfair. But no one ever saw my internal fight. It festered until I realized, much later, that the burden of resentment was heavy and had filled up my backpack. It was no longer worth carrying the weight, and I had to release it.

In rare moments of insight, I willingly and gratefully accepted my role as a wiseman. I would think about wisemen in the grand scheme of life and realize they were uniquely prepared for their role. But then the moments passed, and I would long, just once, to be Mary. My big break finally came when I was thirty-five and living in Cairo, Egypt, but it came far too late. The live Christmas pageant needed baby Jesus, and my three-month old son Jonathan won the 'who gets to be Baby Jesus' lottery. And so I became Mary, but in a supporting role. Perhaps the way it was always meant to be played.

WHEN I BEGAN to relay stories of my boarding school days to my children, the beginning was always the same. *"Once upon a time there was a little girl who lived far, far away in a country called Pakistan..."* It was a little girl, a far-away land, a 'once upon a time.' The plot would change from that point, launching on a journey that included trains, boats, horse-drawn *tongas*, motor rickshaws, Saturday night movies, roommates, and mean teachers. These bedtime stories were truth told through a memory that had rewritten them through the years. The stories included the important ingredients of midnight feasts: fudge, condensed milk, and Ovaltine. They included camping trips and cats that ran away, evacuation suitcases and train trips. The reality that was mine became a story for my children and later on, for others. I communicated memories of this world through a narrative, so that this world wouldn't die.

Bedtime stories often help a parent make peace with both the past and the present. Lying beside your child on a bed, soft pillows under both heads and the favorite stuffed toy held tightly in their arms as both of you slip into a land where you never grow up, is a perfect recipe for peace and contentment.

In bedtime stories, I could rewrite endings, and by telling these stories, I began to see my own passage through childhood with new eyes. What had seemed at the time to be difficult now faded into the background and the 'laced with grace' memories surfaced, all of them bringing a smile and slight nostalgia. Best of all, as my children would doze off, I was left with my silent thoughts and thankfulness that I had grown up enough to see and hear the story through adult eyes and ears.

Like the bedtime stories I told my own children, bedtimes at boarding school were unique times of growing up and growing faith. My earliest memories of boarding school bedtimes are of painfully long devotions with no stories, but Auntie Eunice changed that. Each night she read a bedtime story, told us a Bible story, and prayed with us. We prayed for teachers and the house parents, for our parents who lived far away and did important work, and every night we would pray for Esther Cutherell. I had never met Esther Cutherell, but I knew that we prayed for Esther because she had a hole in her heart. As a little girl, I couldn't imagine this. A hole in her heart? How is she living? How can she walk around? She was three years younger than me. I didn't understand it, but in my child-heart, I prayed.

Then one day the news came. Esther was better. The hole in her heart was gone. She had surgery and she was alive and well, and one day we would all meet her. There was great rejoicing in our little girl's dorm. Our prayers had worked – a little girl was now well, the hole in her heart was healed. I knew that it was doctors who had helped with the miracle, but that didn't make it any less a miracle in my mind.

After prayer time, we would shuffle off to our rooms in floppy slippers and bathrobes, and climb into bed. Auntie Eunice came bed to bed, tucking us in and kissing us goodnight. I don't know how she managed to give so much love to so many girls, but she did.

This could be why my earliest sense of God being close, of God caring for me as an individual, comes from a bunk bed. Our institutional style dormitory rooms had two, three, or four sets of bunk beds, depending on the size. Sometimes I was on the top bunk, other times I was on the bottom. Our only privacy was found in our bunk beds after lights out. In an unspoken rule of boarding school, the only space we could really claim was our bed. And so I did. I claimed it. My bunk bed held secrets that no one else, not even my best friend, would know. Bunk beds never told secrets. They stored them and kept them safe. There in the dark I could be honest with myself, and tears, joy, or anger could flow.

I was in a bunk bed on the bleak, cold November night when Mom arrived unexpectedly after Stan broke his arm. Years later, when I went through my first heartbreak over a blonde-haired, blue-eyed boy named Jeff Taylor, I cried myself to sleep in a bunk bed. When friends were not talking to me and I miserably laid down my head, willing myself to be somewhere else, I was in a bunk bed. If it was a good day, my thoughts right before sleep were like the sunshine and daisies that filled the summer before monsoon season. If it was a difficult day, my thoughts were as dark as the sky right before the heavens burst and monsoon rains flooded the ground. In that bunk bed, I could finally admit that boarding school life was not easy, that there were times of sorrow and struggle.

And I found God in a bunk bed. In that tiny, private space, my first fervent prayers for comfort went up to an unseen God in a Heaven that seemed far away, and I experienced his comfort and presence. It was in a bunk bed that this unseen God responded, an invisible hand reaching out to comfort a little girl who held fast to a stuffed lamb. There were many ways and places where I believe my faith grew, where I met the big and hard questions of life. One of those places was surely a bunk bed, an icon of sorts, witness to a faith that was written on my heart by God's hand.

Marilyn, 1 week old, February 3, 1960

Held by Polly Brown on board the passenger liner Giulio
Cesare, May 17, 1960

Polly and Ralph Brown with Marilyn (held by Polly), Tom
(held by Ralph), and Stan (right, in the background) on
board the Giulio Cesare May 17, 1960

With Ed, dressed for church, summer 1961

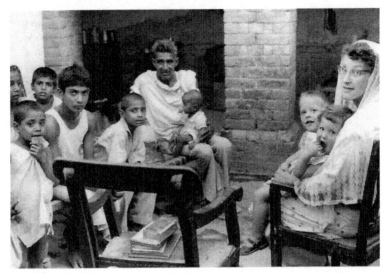

Visiting a Christian family in the villiage of Garhi Yasin,
1962

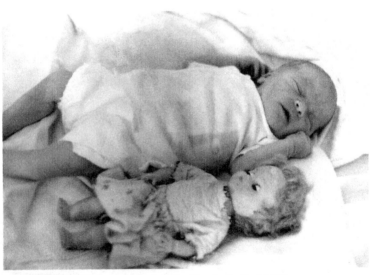

Danny with Marilyn's doll, 1963

Swimming with Tom, Ratodero, 1964

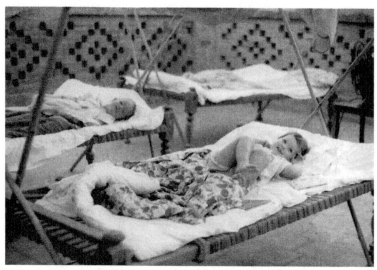

On the rooftop of the house in Ratodero with Tom,
spring 1964

Walking in the park in Hyderabad.
From left: Moeet (friend of Ed and Stan), Ed, Stan,
Tom (just visible), Marilyn, Polly, and Dan

Vacation at Hawkes Bay, 1968
From left: Ed, Stan, Dan, Polly, Marilyn, and Tom

Ed and Sharon's graduation from Gordon College,
Wenham, MA, 1975.
From left: Ruth Kolodinski, Polly, Marilyn, Sharon, Ed,
Dan, Ralph, and Tom

Murree Christian School Cheerleaders in Karachi at an
interschool convention, 1977

Murree Christian School high school banquet with
boyfriend Skip, 1977

Summer 1978, Islamabad airport, leaving Pakistan after
high school graduation

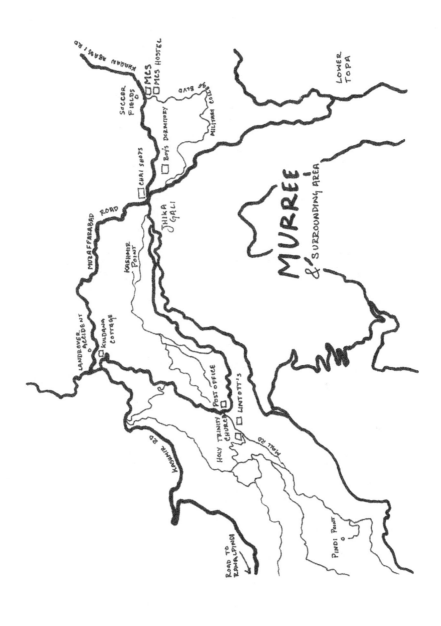

MURREE
& SURROUNDING AREA

KHAGAN ABAS/RD

MCS
MCS HOSTEL
SOCCER FIELDS
Boy's Dormitory
CHAI SHOPS
MILITARY COLLEGE
BLVD

LOWER TOPA

MUZAFFARABAD ROAD
JHIKA GALI
KASHMIR POINT

LANDROVER ACCIDENT
KHADANA COTTAGE

KASHMIR RD

HOLY TRINITY CHURCH
POST OFFICE
LINTOTT'S
MALL RD

PINDI POINT

ROAD TO RAWALPINDI

CHAPTER 3
TONGA RIDES

*Once upon a time, these carriages carried lovely ladies
and the wealthy. Now (year 2002) they carry only trash and
heavy goods.*

Kamat's Potpourri, Carts of India

TONGAS WERE A quintessential part of our world in Sindh, and the clip-clop clip-clop of horses' hooves on asphalt echoes through my memory, arousing longing. At age 16 I wrote to a friend in America: "Three days a week I go and volunteer at a hospital. I go in the morning and a horse-drawn carriage takes me...." A flair for the dramatic and a vivid imagination allowed me to picture myself as a young girl in a Victorian novel being taken through the streets of Shikarpur. In reality, a *tonga* is a simple horse-drawn cart with two large, sturdy wheels that bump along rough, unpaved, dusty streets with large potholes. Before automobiles became common, *tongas* were ubiquitous throughout the subcontinent, and they continue in use in many places. A seat in the front allows a driver to steer the horse; a rear-facing seat holds passengers. A large canopy covers both. Baggage, or hay for the horses, or a combination of baggage and hay, can be stowed under the seat. At home, during school vacations, we travelled by *tonga* daily, observing and being observed by the world around us from our perch on the back seat.

The comforting clip-clop of a *tonga* was the signature sound of school vacations when life slowed to a measured pace. Winter vacation came just when I needed it most. Like hiking a high mountain, imagining I could not go a step farther, boarding school reached a point where I felt I couldn't spend one more day, hour, minute in this place. I had lived with roommates and classmates for three solid months with only the occasional weekend for a break. A bitter December cold had taken the place of crisp fall, and we shivered beside kerosene heaters to try to warm up as best we could. Then, like the miracle of suddenly realizing that you had finally reached the summit, school was over and vacation had begun. I could see the end and knew I could make it.

We packed trunks and *bisters*, tossing dirty clothes in with the clean. The count of underwear, socks, and sweaters was lower than a few months earlier, and everything was more worn and frayed. Soon we would board the sturdy school bus to ride two hours down the mountain to the Rawalpindi train station. I could hardly wait. For this journey, we had no special food packed with a mother's love and tears. We ate bone-dry sandwiches, filled with small traces of peanut butter and jelly or cheddar cheese, made with bread that stuck to the roofs of our mouths. Once on board we yelled out the train windows to summon eager vendors of *puris* and *halwa*, hot *chai* and hard-boiled eggs. To our taste-starved palates, the station platform offered a heavenly buffet, and we quickly tossed our sandwiches out the window, oblivious to the malnourished children we passed each day.

The journey home was subdued – we were tired – and it was long. Those of us who lived in Sindh had the longest route, travelling for eighteen to twenty-four hours. We waved goodbye to classmates at station after station as the train threaded its way through the Punjab. Not many of us were left as we entered the flat, dry landscape of Sindh. With the change of landscape, I realized that our arrival was imminent, and nervous tension filled my stomach. I was so excited but so nervous – nervous to see parents who, but for letters and packages, had been absent for three months, and nervous to interact with siblings who had become strangers.

The train chugged into the station. Tired, smelly bodies jumped out; heavy trunks and stuffed *bisters* were piled onto the station platform. We shyly reunited as a family after three months of separation. Dirty, tired, slightly overwhelmed, we fell into the open arms of our parents. The looks on their faces spoke of pure love and perhaps nervousness as well. We were almost home.

Mom welcomed us with guest towels, china, and favorite meals. We slept in as long as we liked. But Mom never tolerated laziness; after a week, life returned to routine. Five days a week we were up by six-thirty or seven for breakfast – steaming hot bowls of *suji* or *dahlia* with fresh cream and molasses syrup, or eggs and toast made with homemade bread. Mom's cooking was a delectable change from boarding school food.

We each had chores. We all washed clothes, threading them through the old wringer washing machine, fearful lest a finger should slip between the rollers and be crushed. I was the ironing specialist. To this day, I love the transformation of wrinkled to smooth. I labored the longest over my father's white, square, cotton handkerchiefs. Dad seemed to have hundreds of them. I carefully ironed smooth each corner, then, using a spray bottle for steam, I pressed the center of the handkerchief, folded it up in a square, and applied a final touch of the iron to make sure it was perfect. Finally, I placed them on the edge of the ironing board, stacked neat, waiting for my father. It was a methodical task, one that I could easily perform while daydreaming of book characters – Elaine in *Rainbow Garden*, Sarah in *The Little Princess*, Contrary Mary in *The Secret Garden*. So I ironed and dreamed, taking the wrinkled, making it smooth. Ironing dad's handkerchiefs would become a metaphor for the wrinkled problems of life, and for the firm hand of the problem solver whose touch makes wrinkles smooth.

Two afternoons a week, I went visiting with Mom. One of my brothers called for a *tonga* and off we would lurch, carefully draped in *dupattas*, eyes downward – or not. Sometimes I delighted in looking up, looking around me, defiantly, at the sea of men, cars, horses, oxcarts, vendors, machinists, and tire shops that surrounded our home. In adolescence, I enjoyed the attention, imagining myself a mysterious foreigner whom everyone we passed wanted to meet. In reality, I was awkward, a chubby adolescent who nevertheless believed I was beautiful even at my most graceless stages.

We were welcomed with great hospitality to the homes of friends, and into their inner courtyards and tea times. The inner sanctum of the courtyard was a women's world, a world where *burqas* were put aside and *dupattas* taken from heads and secured around necks. This was where real life happened, where women talked about babies, birth control, husbands, scandal, neighbor gossip, food, and relatives. Conversation was in Urdu or Sindhi, and I followed along, periodically interrupting Mom to ask for clarification or remind her to tell her friends something that I wanted them to know. As I grew older, the daughters of Mom's friends became my friends, and our conversations became deeper and more honest.

Our friends came from every socioeconomic level, and their homes and habitats reflected their material status. Sometimes our visits took place in Christian slums where one-room mud houses sat side by side with round, brown cow manure patties on the outside walls, drying to provide the family with fuel to cook over open fires. Other times we would be ushered through small side doors into large courtyards surrounded by rooms with opulent furniture covered in plastic. Still other times we would be visiting in middle class homes in the center of the city. We would sit on plastic-clad sofas, pictures hung high above us along the walls.

There was equal diversity in religions. We would visit in Hindu homes, Muslim homes, and Christian homes. As foreigners, we had an advantage in being seen as "other" – an advantage that allowed us much freedom in communicating across religion and culture. We were aligned with no one, and it allowed us to form friendships with many different women.

It was the inner courtyards of Muslim women where I had the most fun, where my curiosity, empathy, and respect grew.

In this inner sanctum, and the oldest woman was usually in command, her word was law. Those inner courtyard moments offered a small window into some of the workings of Pakistani society. Courtyards were the domain of strong women, women who lived their lives under the shadows of minarets and husbands, women seen as oppressed by the outside world. I never saw the oppression. I saw color and life, spices and personality.

Though the homes and people were different, the visits followed the same routine. We would arrive and small talk would begin: the weather, the children, sometimes local events. The conversation then moved on into deeper topics. What was really going on with the children, who was pregnant, who couldn't get pregnant. "Could one of your doctors help?" was sometimes asked. Often the relationships had first been forged at the hospital during a moment of crisis.

That was certainly the case with my friend Jamila. She had ended up at the hospital unable to get pregnant and was diagnosed with pelvic inflammatory disease. The cause? Untreated sexually transmitted diseases, probably acquired from a husband's business trip to a large city. These sensitive areas were difficult to navigate. In Jamila's case, there was a happy ending, at least in terms of pregnancy. She was treated with antibiotics and got pregnant soon afterwards. I would see her again several years later, and she would be shaking her head in despair, asking me how she could prevent another pregnancy. After her first child, she produced three more babies in three years. She was tired.

As we talked, we would drink steaming cups of tea and eat special savory and sweet treats. Hot, fresh *pakoras, samosa* with special chutney, and my favorites – *gulab jamuns,* a round, rust-colored, donut-like sweet that was soaked in a sugar syrup. As the afternoon went on, my mom was sensitive to the chores of the household and would ask permission to leave. "So soon?" they would say. But we knew it was simply hospitality. There was a lot to do to prepare for the evening meal, and we'd best be on our way. We would leave as the late afternoon sun was setting, the silhouettes of palm trees outlined against a red-gold sky. As the *tonga* approached our door, echoes of the call to prayer would begin. We had left one world, and were entering into the world our family created within our four walls.

This women's world was extended into the *zenana* section of the bazaar. Every bazaar had an area that was for women only. The shopkeepers were men, but other men were excluded. Beyond the curtain of a shop, *burqas* could be thrown off and we would watch as bolts of bright-colored silks, satins, and cotton were strewn across counter tops. Chatter about weddings and events mingled with fierce bargaining for the best prices. I learned early to bargain. I have never become reconciled to paying a set price.

Sindh was conservative; *purdah* was almost universally observed. *Purdah* segregated women from men who were not part of the family, and ensured that women's bodies were covered to protect from the eyes of men who were not in their family or community, and therefore not welcome. Each time I returned to Sindh, I stepped into this system and, with it, into a way of life. I dressed and acted like those around me, wearing the latest styles of *shalwar, chemise,* and *dupatta.*

I learned early how to buy cloth and drape a *dupatta*. While I might have looked the part, my skin was pale and my laugh was loud. When I went to the bazaar with girlfriends, they shushed me, embarrassed of the attention I drew. Religion ordered life, and modesty was part of that order. In my teen years, we covered ourselves with long Iranian *chadors*, half circles of patterned rayon that draped beautifully over our bodies. One of the biggest compliments of my adult years was when I once wore Pakistani clothes in Chicago and a young Pakistani man remarked that he could tell I was raised in Pakistan because I wore them with such ease.

Later I saw that I didn't learn as much as I could have, as much as I should have, during these times in the inner courtyard. Initially I was a child, queen of my own universe. Rather than listen closely to stories from Pakistanis, I would be restless and want them to know who I was, what was important to me. When I became a teenager, I was more aware, though still egocentric. During those years I began to ask more questions and see each woman as an individual with a story. I paid more attention and my curiosity turned into respect, later producing empathy. How I long to go back and relive those moments, to ask more questions, to understand better. It was only after leaving Pakistan that I really recognized what a privilege it was to spend time in the inner courtyards, to glimpse a life that those born and bred in the West would never experience.

LIKE THE INNER courtyards of our friends' homes, the Shikarpur Christian Hospital compound was a space where women ruled. The hospital was run by female doctors, midwives, nurses, and teachers, and served female patients. A gifted doctor, Dr. Maybel Bruce, realized early in her medical career in Pakistan that the medical needs of women in Sindh were too great for a mobile clinic. Out of her vision a hospital was born and grew into a sanctuary where dedicated doctors saved the lives of women who defied textbook theory and lived under circumstances and situations where they should have died. It became a secure place where healthy babies were born to proud mamas; where women's lives were saved when deliveries became complicated; where women came to be treated for the pelvic inflammatory diseases they acquired when their husbands left town and went to the big city. Their bodies bore the cost of a husband's unfaithfulness.

Because of the work of the hospital, Shikarpur naturally became a central location for missionaries to live. Almost all of the missionary families in Shikarpur were somehow connected to the hospital. Doctors, nurses, pharmacists, and administrators all lived either on the hospital compound or in close proximity.

Periodically, someone would talk about the old days; days when Shikarpur was a beautiful city with gardens, roses, and large homes gracing the streets. It was a banking city, a financial capital strategically located because of its accessibility from Central and West Asia. History tells of a city with culture, trade, architecture, and green space. Shikarpur was described as the capital of "merchants, money changers, and bankers."

When Pakistan gained independence from India and established itself as a separate Muslim nation, hundreds of thousands of Hindus were displaced and journeyed to India to begin a new life. Just as Hindus left, Muslims entered and Shikarpur continued to grow.

I don't know when Shikarpur began to lose its beauty and former glory. Part of the change came with partition and strained relations with India, but well before that time of transition and war, the city was not what it had been in the 1800s. A time where horse-drawn Victorian carriages carried the wealthy to the Shahi Bagh gardens; a time when bankers completed business deals in high-ceilinged villas; a time when there was a zoo that had cheetahs, lions, and wild boar.

This was a Shikarpur I never knew. While walking through the bazaar, if I looked up, I could see faint glimpses of the former glory in old, beautifully-crafted windows. But eventually my eyes would have to shift downward and take in the surroundings at eye level. Eye level brought me back to the present, and the glory of the past was no longer visible.

While I never saw the Shikarpur of that time, it was still a special place for me. Our family was always welcomed with great joy, and we kids saw it as a place of vacation and fun, a place where there were others who were like us: missionary families living between worlds.

FROM THE TIME I was four years old, playing with my hard-earned doctor set, I wanted to be a nurse. I wanted to work with people around healthcare needs. I wanted to sit with them in their illness, walk them through their pain. My desire strengthened as I observed the inner workings of Shikarpur Christian Hospital. In my final two years of high school I officially volunteered, learning how to work in a busy outpatient clinic, weighing and measuring moms and babies, helping give shots to children.

The hospital was known throughout the district as a place of *baraka*, of blessing. In the local Civil Hospital good care was difficult to find, and patients were treated according to income level. This hospital was different. "You care about us!" the women would say repeatedly. Any foreigner seen in those parts was immediately thought to belong to the hospital. You could walk in the bazaar and have a woman fully veiled in a *burqa* stop you, asking when the hospital was next open, asking if you would deliver her sister's baby. The hospital was a lifeline, a beacon of good practice and caring staff.

The hospital compound housed clinics, exam rooms, and patient wards. Toward the rear gate there were also large buildings with separate apartments for expatriate medical staff and a dormitory for single Pakistani nurses. As I grew older, the dormitory became a place of friendship and learning, as most of the nurses were only slightly older than me.

Because I saw and absorbed so much from the hospital and its core of devoted women and men, the nursing profession almost chose me. The hospital's inner workings were familiar to me. I knew the inpatient ward where *charpais* were placed in a straight row on both sides of a low wall. I knew the courtyard where family members would camp out, making meals and tea for their sick relatives. I knew the private rooms, where the wealthier of the area came for medical care. Before the hospital officially opened, I raced with friends and siblings up and down the chipped marble corridors, dodging adults who appeared out of nowhere to tell us to calm down.

On winter vacations in my junior and senior years of high school, the hospital became part of my weekly routine. Three days a week, I left our house after breakfast, wearing *chador* and *dupatta,* to volunteer at the outpatient clinic. In a small room off the outpatient waiting room I recorded the weights of moms and babies and of pregnant and postpartum women on paper cards in small, neat handwriting. I gave injections with glass syringes that had been pre-sterilized, along with rubber gloves and needles, in giant autoclaves. I grasped tongs, picked up the needle, and attached it to the glass syringe. I swabbed the container of fluid with a small, alcohol-soaked cotton ball, and inserted the needle, carefully extracting the required amount. This was my introduction to sterile technique. When I arrived in the United States to begin my nursing program, I would discover that these methods were primitive, and I was met by surprise and disbelief when I told my fellow students what I had learned.

These opportunities were a gift that I didn't fully appreciate until I embarked on my career. Two dedicated nurse midwives, Auntie Hannah and Auntie Phyllis, mentored me. Both had hearts that overflowed with love for the women and children of the Indus Valley. They were the finest nurses I have known. Outpatient clinic ended in early or mid-afternoon, depending on what emergencies came through the dusty roads and arrived at the gates of the hospital compound, and I would make my way home, tired but ready to grow my imagination through afternoon play.

The health needs in upper Sindh were overwhelming. Hospitals were often a last resort, and our doctors and nurses saw medical problems that were rare and almost unbelievable. Too often, families brought women in too late, only to die on arrival. This was where I first encountered a woman with a fistula, an opening between her bladder and vagina, a result of delayed delivery, a small pelvis, and poor obstetrical care. It is impossible to forget the overpowering smell of leaking urine, and the look of desperation and resignation on the face of a young woman, probably only a few years older than I, who was facing suffering and social isolation. I also encountered guilt – why her not me? What had I done to deserve a life of privilege, a life where I was a prized only daughter, applauded and beloved? I faced anger at conditions that put a woman at such risk. Social justice was not a word that was used to gain political or spiritual points; it was a reality for those who worked in Pakistan, an outpouring of love of God extended towards those with needs of every sort.

Seen against the vast need, the hospital was like a band-aid on an oozing, massive wound. Later in life, my stories of Shikarpur Christian Hospital would be criticized by "enlightened" westerners with no use for missionary doctors and nurses and scornful of such band-aid approaches. But a band-aid makes a huge difference to the person suffering from the wounds. The staff at the hospital took the time to care, to clean, to treat, to protect. Any care given at this hospital was given in the name of Jesus, a name that all the staff – whether Pakistani, Canadian, Dutch, American, or Australian – believed to have authority and power. It was a name and person known by both Christians and Muslims, though different attributes were given to this name: to one the way to God, a Savior, to the other a great prophet, to both someone of great importance. So the band-aids were given in Jesus' name, and physical lives were saved, building a reputation that spread throughout the area. When I returned many years later to work on a flood-relief team based out of the hospital, its reputation had only grown. People continued to wait for hours to receive care within its walls, a sanctuary, and a refuge in a hurting world.

THE PAKISTANI, AMERICAN, British, and Australian women who shaped my life and faith each have a separate place in my memory. My own mom, through every developmental stage of my life, showed me patience, compassion, and unconditional love. She became my favorite feminist, a woman who was not content to know how to read herself, but taught other women to read around her worn kitchen table, somehow fitting it in amidst her skinning of chickens, paying of bills, boiling of milk, and yelling at *chowkidars,* the men who would guard our house and run errands to the bazaar. Mom was and is smart, strong, and articulate. She gave birth to five children, and she read aloud to them before they had finished breast-feeding. Mom raised me to believe women were amazing and could do anything, even in a male-dominated society where women were rarely seen outside the home.

Auntie Betty Addleton, mother of my best friend Nancy, could make a mud hut look like a mansion. As her friends struggled with peeling concrete walls and salts eating through paint leaving stained blotches, Betty covered the walls floor to ceiling with expertly-made drapes. Using paint, creativity, and ingenuity, Betty created magic in her home, shaping spaces of rest and escape, oases from the heat and chaos. After visiting Nancy, I always left filled with creative ideas, returning home to rearrange the furniture, make pillows for the bed, and create beauty. Betty taught me that beauty could be created in unimagineable spaces, and that such beauty was to be shared and celebrated.

Dr. Mary Wilder, a brilliant doctor, was as funny and quick-witted as she was compassionate. I was in awe of her brain, but so comfortable with her personality that I never feared her. Auntie Hannah Leutbeche, who ended sentences with "eh" in honor of her adopted Canadian home, became like an older sister to us. Every year she came on our family vacation to the beach in Karachi. Auntie Hannah was pretty and fun, always willing to play games and try things with us, and was one of Mom's best friends. Auntie Connie Johnson was petite and Swedish, mother to four sons, two of whom were my close friends. Auntie Connie dropped everything to welcome people into her home. She had a laugh that was bigger than she was, and a heart that honored all. Dr. Carol

Hover was strength personified, single-parenting her four children after the tragic death of her husband, and loving so many so well.

Martha Domji, daughter of an influential Marwari convert to Christianity, was my age, and her spirit and sense of humor were like mine. Despite language differences, we had no barriers in our communication. Martha became my soulmate, my *Anne of Green Gables* "kindred spirit." Angel, Elizabeth, and Soraya, all a few years older than me, extended generous offers of friendship. Though female and Christian in a land where both those things were strikes against them, both Angel and Elizabeth became doctors. This was a tribute to their brains and resilience. Sadly, Soraya died of breast cancer when she was barely in her thirties.

As I got older, Muslim friends were also a part of my world. There was Jamila, married young and unable to get pregnant; Arbab, a gifted seamstress, sewing clothes so that all four of her children could go on to college, despite the fact that she had only attended a few grades of school; and Hajirah, Arbab's sister, unmarried and highly educated, a classy Sindhi woman who taught children at a school during the mornings and language to missionary women during the afternoons. There was another Arbab, a Brahui woman living on the grounds of the Holland Bungalow, soft-spoken and lovely, chiding me that I looked ugly every time my skin became brown from beach sun. I would laugh and tell her that I wanted to look like her. It was true. When I reached high school, I never thought I looked Pakistani enough and always wanted my skin to be browner. My only chance to work at this was at the beach every year. Soon after, I would head back to school in Murree where the tan quickly faded in the cool of the mountains. Although the same age as me physically, Arbab was years older in experience and wisdom.

She had birthed three babies by the time I turned 18. I was a petulant child; she was a woman of valor.

All of these women were amazing in their own right, modeling grace and wisdom as they lived out their faith as minorities, as woman, or as both. These were my models, strong women with hearts open to love God and the world. They did not preach or chastise, but they lived out loud a faith that worked its way into my heart and soul.

During some of our years of living in Larkana, home to the famous Bhutto family, there were no other foreigners in our town, just our family. Pakistani school schedules differed from ours, so our neighbors were in school while we were on vacation. On weekends, we went to church and visited church families. On slow weekday afternoons, Mom and I would go visiting. The rest of the time, we had our imaginations and our books.

We were never bored. After chores were completed each day I had books, games, and brothers bursting with creative ideas. A hot air balloon was one of these, a work of art, painstakingly pieced together from squares of tissue paper. The finished product was six feet by four feet. We attached wires to the bottom, joining them in the center to hold the flame that would send it soaring into the air. Construction took a long time, and every day I looked to see what progress had been made. I was not allowed to participate in the making of the balloon, but the truth is, being impatient with details, I would have quickly tired of the care with which it was being assembled.

Launch day finally came. We gathered excitedly as Stan lit the flame. We watched the balloon rise up, up, up into the cloudless blue sky of Sindh. Then, after climbing a couple of hundred meters, a gust of wind fanned the flame, the balloon wobbled, the tissue paper caught on fire, and we watched aghast as a flaming ball of fire hurtled straight toward the petrol station across from our house. Hearts beating fast, my brothers ran to find the remains while townspeople gathered, staring up at the sky in awe and, perhaps, terror. No one was hurt and nothing blew up, but clearly the hot air balloon needed a design check. Not easily defeated, my brothers began work on a second.

Our environment fostered imagination and Mom encouraged it. I lived in my books, taking on each character, acting them out in my head. In a single day, I was a Swiss girl in a boarding school in the Alps, a young woman in South Africa, or solving mysteries as Nancy Drew. Reading opened the world to me, and I would walk around, immersed in my inner dialogue. In my imagination, I could be anyone and anywhere.

Mom also read aloud to us in the evenings, on car trips, and on picnics beside the canal bank. She put planning and effort into those picnics. To make a picnic lunch in Sindh, Mom had to bake bread, make mayonnaise from scratch, hard boil eggs in time to cool, make cookies, buy fruit and wash it in iodine solution, and more. These were major events. Finally, with a basket packed full of homemade sandwiches, carrot sticks, hardboiled eggs, and a famous chocolate wacky cake (also known as "Depression Cake" because it was made with no eggs and no milk) we would head off in late afternoon, Mom dragging Dad away from work at his overloaded desk.

Picnics were time away from compounds, visiting, and the endless interruptions that were a part of everyday life. Sitting together on an old blanket spread over the dry brush of the canal bank, we were alone as a family. After eating and talking, Mom always brought out a book. She read us *The Chosen* and *The Promise* by Chaim Potok, *The Chronicles of Narnia* by C.S. Lewis, and *The Glad Season* by Paula Elizabeth

Sutts, about a boy growing up with his grandmother in the far north of Canada. The stories enriched our lives, and all five of us siblings are still avid readers.

Another outing that sparked our imaginations was to the ancient city of Mohenjo-Daro, whose name means "Mound of the Dead" in Sindhi. It is incredible that we picnicked amidst the ruins of one of the great urban centers of the Indus Valley Civilization, picking through artifacts as if it was a children's playground. In 1980, two years after I graduated from high school, Mohenjo-Daro was declared a UNESCO World Heritage Site, but as children, we had no idea how important it was to the world of archaeology. We laughed at the flocks of tourists that would come on buses with the latest cameras from Hong Kong over their shoulders. This was home. Why would anyone want to take so many pictures? Of course, we took our own pictures. That was different. That was to record a memory, to remind ourselves of our time together, our outing, our special place. It had nothing to do with the fame of the area.

Mohenjo-Daro's ancient bricks delineated areas where houses and thriving communities once stood, and my friends and I imagined we were transported back to that day, ancient, beautiful young women, long hair flowing, and the eyes of every ancient young man in the region on us, vying for our love. Mom had her own reasons for imagining. As we would walk through the ruins, I remember her rueful observation that this ancient city had closed sewers. In the twentieth century cities where we lived, raw sewage flowed in narrow, shallow, open trenches throughout the cities. I would not know the significance of this until later in my life, when I realized that many of the most common diseases in the area could have been avoided with closed sewers.

Kot Diji Fort was another favorite family outing. Kot Diji, built in the early seventeenth century, was 25 miles east of the Indus River and strategically built at the edge of the desert to give its occupants prior warning of approaching enemies. The fort was protected by a massive wall and huge iron gates. We knew almost every room, and would race through it as though it were nothing special. Just inside the gates, a deep well with an enormous unguarded opening left me with nightmares after our visits. My fear of falling in that well, though unspoken, was acute.

My sister-in-law once remarked that elementary school education is wasted on the young. These outings were like that, their significance lost in their normalcy and the frequency with which we visited. I did not care that Mohenjo-Daro or Kot Diji Fort were archaeological treasures. I was a child, and as a child these places were there for my pleasure, for our family outings. In later years these places increased in importance to me, but with a sad irony: as I appreciated their archeological importance, I was left with simply a photograph and a memory, unable to visit and without anyone who cared to hear my stories of a remarkable childhood that was so unremarkable to me.

So it was that at the end of a day of walking through the ruins of Mohenjo-Daro or Kot Diji, we made our way home under a dark, cloudless sky filled with stars. I would fall asleep, tired, but full and satisfied, dreaming of ancient things, lost civilizations, and the importance of closed sewers.

Summers we vacationed in the Swat and Kaghan Valleys. Both were astonishingly beautiful and untrammeled. We effortlessly traversed swinging footbridges swaying far above rushing rivers, glorying in our immortal youth, oblivious to the danger. Tall mountains towered over these river valleys, their heights covered with meringue-like peaks of snow. We sometimes camped, sometimes booked government rest houses. We hiked beside rivers, savored delicious kebabs roasted over open fires, and ended each night reading by the light of a hissing pressure lantern.

Each winter we spent our most significant family times at Hawke's Bay in Karachi. Bladen Wilmer Hawke, the ninth Baron Hawke of Towton, set up the first cottage on this beach in the 1930s. The beach was named for him, and Hawke's Bay became an affectionate household word that still brings a sigh of deep gratitude and unappeased yearning. Though only a week long, these vacations gave so much rest and joy that they seemed longer. Our family would sign up for a beach week in late January or early February when the weather had cast off the cool of winter and we could be certain of sunshine and warmth.

We left on the 300-mile, eight-hour trip before the sun came up, amidst the sounds of oxcarts and the early morning *muezzin*, lurching off in a Land Rover filled to the brim with kids, supplies, bedding, clothes, books, and Auntie Hannah. We reached Karachi in the afternoon, stopping in the city to load up on supplies, impatient for the ocean. Royal palm trees lined the road to Hawke's Bay, and we could smell the ocean long before it came into view. The week was filled with the best that vacation offers. For a family never shy of fighting, that week was always surprisingly harmonious. We played, rested, and read together. Maybe it was the magic of Auntie Hannah's presence, maybe it was the magic of the beach, maybe both and more.

Sometimes we watched the struggle of a mama green sea turtle lumbering up the beach in the moonlight. While for us the beach was full of people and fun, for this turtle it was a long, lonely walk. These turtles were massive, weighing hundreds of pounds, and the journey from sea to land was not only arduous because of their size, but also because she had traveled so many miles to get there.

Once on land, the turtle lumbered far up the beach, laboriously excavated a hole big enough to lay about 80 eggs, covered it with sand, and camouflaged it as if it had already been disturbed and nothing had been found, aiming to trick predators into believing there was nothing there. Finally, exhausted, she struggled her way back to the ocean, resting her heavy, weary body, allowing the ocean waves of the Arabian Sea to carry her away. She would never know that she was observed, watched by a family unknown to her, staying in a small hut nearby. She would never know the life lessons she taught, the quiet that would come upon a noisy bunch so that we wouldn't disturb her important work.

If we were lucky, we watched the baby green sea turtles hatch, struggling their way across the sand to the ocean. A lone dog might alert us of their arrival, sniffing at a pile of dirt, frantically digging. We ran, shouted, and waved the dog off, fiercely protective. These baby turtles were much as we were: vulnerable and small. They faced a big, dangerous world, and their struggle was overwhelming. Make it to the ocean. Survive. Grow. Thrive. Growing up in Pakistan was a bit like being a baby sea turtle. Pakistan and the small community we were a part of cocooned us for a while, and then we had to go; we had to make it in a world that could be hostile to who we were and what we believed. While in Pakistan, we had parents and a community that warned off those that might cause harm, but we too had to make our journey to and across the sea. And in many ways, we made it alone.

I never tired of watching baby turtles make their way to the sea, but I didn't understand their lesson until later. As children, gathered around, we were frantic to help. We did not yet understand that it was critically important for these turtles to struggle their way to the ocean without help; the lonely journey across the sand is a turtle's first step in gaining the strength to survive.

That my parents took the time to take us on picnics and outings critically shaped our sense of family and our sense of self in relation to the family. At every crossroad, two worlds intersected: the broader world of a mission community and work in Pakistan and the smaller world of us, the Browns. We were molded and shaped by both: parents who loved us first and Pakistan second. Parents who were called to a God who had entrusted them with five children. We watched some of our friends become lost in the shadows, lost to well-meaning parents with a calling. We were not. We were loved through reading and picnics, through outings to ancient sites and running through forts, through creative play, through dinnertime discussions.

We were also loved through pets. There was Frisky and then there were a series of 'Old Black Cats' (OBC we called them), and the stories and memories of our pets meld into one another. Stories of cats giving birth and tiny kittens; cats running away and being found – or not; and cats traveling throughout the country in a sturdy Land Rover. There was the time when our cat ran away – we were certain she heard our conversation the night before about leaving for America, and, knowing her beloved family was leaving, would have none of it. There was the time when she followed us on a hiking trip in the Kaghan Valley; the time when, frightened by a friend's dog, she jumped out of a window and ran into the night – only to be found in a place that housed sacred Hindu cows.

In recent years, our cat stories came into print form – Mom wrote a book called *Cat Tales*. The book chronicles our cats and our family adventures with these cats. Mom loved our cats – all of them. She would go to remarkable lengths to make sure the cats were safe and well cared for. In my earliest letters from home, I ask a lot of questions about our cat: *"How is Frisky?"* I ask. *"Tell Frisky 'hi' for me."* *"What has Frisky been up to?"* The only thing I show more affection for is my younger brother, Danny.

When Mom wrote the book, I felt like I had a window into her experience as a mom in a way I never had before. The book about our cats felt as much about her as it did about our pets. Through the escapades of our cat I saw more of what it was for her to trust, to fear, to wonder if she and my dad were foolishly putting a family in danger, away from any relatives and thousands of miles from where she and Dad had grown up.

Mom and Dad weren't perfect, but somehow, by grace, they gave us what we needed to grow healthy and whole. We grew in faith and imagination, we grew in compassion and discipline, and we were never lost to a bigger mission. We were a vital part of both of these intersecting worlds. Family picnics, outings, and pets were an essential part of why we were never lost.

THE ADDLETONS WERE always part of my life. Betty was gracious and beautiful; Hu, personable and handsome. They were southerners, natives of Georgia, gifted in relationships and clear in their call. We each had a best friend in the Addleton family: David and Stan; Jonathan and Tom; and beautiful, dark-haired, dark-eyed Nancy would surely have been my best friend forever, my BFF, if the term had been invented. We were partners in crime, confidantes about everything. Nancy was as close to a princess as any of my friends could be.

My memories of Nancy begin at age four. She was to spend the weekend at Mount Pleasant, our ironically-named house in Murree with its leaky roof, pungent commode, and well-worn furniture. A high fever cancelled our sleepover, but Nancy's clothes had already been delivered to my house. Oh how I loved her clothes. In my feverish state I imagined that by some act of God the clothes would be mine to keep, or that, in a fit of generosity, Nancy and Auntie Betty had given them to me. When I woke next morning, fever-free, the clothes were gone and my best friend was staying with someone else.

Nancy, with her cute black poodle, Dixie, her go-go boots, and her southern charm, was a constant in my early life. We talked about boys and made no-bake cookies. I marveled at her flair for decorating and her paint-splattered wastebaskets. We leafed through a book about the Beatles, shouting 'mine' every time we came to a picture of George Harrison. We shared boarding school joys and miseries, got mononucleosis at the same time, and had to leave boarding early, and oohed and aahed at her red velvet 9th grade banquet dress. We spent every winter vacation together in Sindh, and this meant time with the whole Addleton family. We stayed up so late that Auntie Betty had to reprimand us, and laughed so hard about silly things that we cried. We did all the things that best friends are supposed to do.

We dreamed of returning to the U.S. together to attend Emory University, where we would wear miniskirts in defiance of the Murree Christian School dress code. I left Pakistan to spend ninth grade in the United States. One year stretched to two. We wrote each other continuously, and it was a wonderful day when I came back from school to find a blue aerogram from Nancy, reassurance that somewhere in the world I was not a cultural misfit. I always had Nancy.

Until she was no longer there. When I returned to Pakistan, Nancy was gone.

Friendships formed in our small community were and are unique. We forged relationships with likely and unlikely people, and they occupied our hearts and souls. Together we faced birth, death, tragedy, sickness, political instability, separation from blood relatives, car accidents, boarding school, tension in relationships, food rations, and so much more.

These memories and events were woven together into an immense tapestry. But unless cared for, a tapestry gets loose threads, and those threads can unravel into holes – holes of too many goodbyes, unraveling of loss. We push the losses aside, dismiss the goodbyes as just part of life, part of being third culture kids. But buried losses don't stay buried. Like a submarine, they eventually surface, and we realize that they were never gone. So our griefs, our goodbyes, would surface later in life, like angry monsters demanding a redo of the goodbyes, demanding time to grieve the losses, demanding another chance. But we get only one chance at childhood. When that childhood is lived thousands of miles and oceans away from the place you live as an adult, you can't go back. When our childhood is good and filled with a sense of wonder, it outweighs the pain and grief that came along the way. We may long to recreate it, perhaps because in it we see something of what the world should be, what the world could be. But recreating it is an impossibility, and in our case, even revisiting the places and people was impossible.

EVERY VACATION FROM the time I was ten years old, Mom encouraged me to study Urdu. She tried to teach me herself, bought me children's books to learn the script, cajoled, pleaded, and threatened. It did no good. I had every opportunity to learn this rich language, and I squandered it. My regret has lasted a lifetime.

My brothers could naturally learn and practice Urdu in the bazaars. They had freedom to wander, to talk to shop keepers, to make friendships outside the walls of our home. My opportunities were more limited. Visits were not spontaneous but had to be pre-planned. A note had to be sent to friends. "Could we visit?" Mom would ask. The reply might come a day or two later. My brothers had none of these restrictions, and their language abilities reflect this.

Like so many things in childhood, I didn't know what I had until I lost it. I didn't recognize the importance of being bilingual until I was in high school. By that time, I had only two years left in school, and a busy social life in English, my language of friendship, love, and popularity. I squandered opportunities to learn, opting instead to flirt, gossip, and share in English. I was a teenager. It didn't matter where in the world I was, my highest priorities were popularity, friendships, talking, and boys – not always in that order. While I could have been conjugating verbs and learning more vocabulary, I was instead busy with a social life with friends, and a vivid imagination when alone. My Urdu became "fossilized" so that I would never get past a certain point and would repeatedly make the same mistakes. Even as I lament this, I understand it. As children we make decisions based on the immediate.

It is the rare child that thinks ahead and realizes that they might grow to regret some of their decisions. I was not that rare child.

It was on vacations that I had the most contact with Pakistanis. During the school year I lived in a world of international expatriate friends: Margo from Canada, Carol from Australia, Jenny from New Zealand, Elizabeth from Scotland. Their names evoke a kaleidoscope of memories from my boarding school years. But during school vacation, our family participated in the local church made up of Punjabi Christians who had migrated their way to the Sindh area and formed small communities that lived and worshiped together. I was acutely aware of living between two worlds when I attended church services while on school vacations. When young, I was not always good at making friends with Pakistanis, feeling insecure in my language skills and growing more introverted as a result. This sometimes elicited bad behavior.

Like the incident when I stuck my tongue out at the two Pakistani teenagers after church, resulting in the hardest spanking I ever received, there were other times where I wore superiority and privilege like it was my right. I bow my head in shame at these memories. As much as I felt I belonged in Pakistan, I was a guest, and my parents would not tolerate rude behavior. Not deterred by my occasionally-bad behavior and immaturity, my parents continued to invite Pakistanis of every economic level to our home, sometimes serving several dozen cups of tea in a day. They modeled friendship and love through hospitality and cups of tea. In this way, I learned, friendships are made and discussion and disagreement go down easy, swallowed with the creamy chai made with buffalo milk and the crunchy goodness of Digestive Biscuits.

DAILY DEVOTIONS WERE the spiritual food that my parents relied on. It was bread and water to them. The first thing I saw when I peeked in my parents' room every morning was Dad on his knees beside an unmade bed, pouring his heart out to his Creator, his Redeemer, dare I say – his Friend. Mom and Dad were a window to a bigger picture, a picture of redemption and restoration.

Mom and Dad urged us to create our own patterns of communicating with God. Praying, reading the Bible, reflecting in a journal – all of this was encouraged. When I was young, that was fine. It was part of life. But as I grew older, I wearied of this expectation. I was not interested. I could think of far better and more captivating activities. Why pick up my boring Bible when right beside my bed was a Nancy Drew book in which I knew she would find the murderer and once again be the heroine of her own series? Why would I want to read stories about people with names like Enoch or Sampson or Nathaniel when I could read stories about Darrell Rivers and nasty spiteful Gwendoline at a boarding school called *Mallory Towers* in Cornwall?

The books that captured my imagination seemed far more useful in my world than any Old Testament character could possibly be. I found no boarding school stories in the Bible with gossipy girls and a heroine who put them in their place. *Mallory Towers* seemed far more practical than the Bible. I could not yet see that the remarkable stories of deeply flawed biblical characters told the great story of redemption. I had not yet learned that the phrase "But God…" anticipates a divine intervention in the broken mess of humanity. I had not yet experienced the great hope I found later in words of Scripture. Instead, I saw red-letter boring wrapped up in black binding.

Dad would pop his head into my bedroom and jovially say, "Good morning Marilyn! How are you? Having your devotions?" And so I learned to deceive. I picked up my *Mallory Towers*, wrapped it in my bedclothes, and read away to my heart's content, albeit with a prickly conscience. He would come and pose the question, and I, with a guilty smile, would nod even as I read about Gwendoline making Darrell cry and spreading vicious rumors throughout *Mallory Towers*.

I became adept at deceiving, brilliant at people pleasing. I skillfully delivered what I knew people wanted, regardless of its truth. This was, in part, a survival skill, learned and honed to perfection in boarding school. But discovering the long-term effects of this pattern was critical in my spiritual formation. I perfected my ability to deceive under the bedclothes during vacation. I repented of the same at many different points through my life.

Yet through these years, my faith grew deep roots from a father who modeled discipline and obedience, from a mother who modeled trust and love, from a community that, though desperately imperfect, knew forgiveness and second chances. I learned that deceit practiced under blankets with books can and is forgiven. I learned that, as amazing as *Mallory Towers*, *The Bobbsey Twins*, and *The Chosen* were, the stories woven through the Bible would form in me truth claims that would never die.

Chapter 4
Bus Trips

*Life is similar to a bus ride. The journey begins when we
board the bus. We meet people along our way of which some are
strangers, some friends and some strangers yet to be friends.
There are stops at intervals and people board in. At times some
of these people make their presence felt, leave an impact through
their grace and beauty on us fellow passengers while on other
occasions they remain indifferent.*

Chirag Tulsiani

THE SIGHT OF brightly painted buses crowded with double the people they can physically seat is as common to residents of Pakistan as it is shocking to visitors. Bright red, pink, orange, yellow, and blue flowers, paisley designs, yellow suns and moons, pictures of voluptuous women -- all these find their artsy home on these buses. People hang out of doors, windows, and sit on the roofs as these buses barrel down dangerous roads. A road might have high walls of rock on one side, cliffs that plunge hundreds of feet down mountains on the other, but buses travel on, oblivious to the certain death an accident would bring.

The history of bus and truck art dates back to the British Raj. In the 1920's a bus company commissioned a group of artisans under the leadership of a man named Ustad Elahi Bakhsh to paint buses so that the company could attract more passengers.

Recently, the United States discovered this art form, and the Smithsonian Museum in Washington, D.C., now features a truck painted with the classic colors, symbols, and designs commonly seen in the Indian subcontinent.

Despite globalization and the occasional cultural erosion that comes with it, bus art has survived. Satellite dishes may be found on the roofs of remote village houses and cell phones far from cities, but bus art still brightens the landscape of the country.

My early adolescent years in Pakistan were like these busses. They are brilliant with colorful, passionate drawings depicting love and life on their bodies. But it was the plainest bus in the country that was an ever-present part of my passage through Pakistan: the Murree Christian School Bus. This army-green bus had *Murree Christian School* in bold lettering across both sides. The emblem was painted in solid white beside the letters. It was iconic, a symbol of our school and my upbringing.

This old school bus could tell stories of a five-year old child with thick, dark hair in a pixie cut, crying because she forgot her bus stop on the first day of kindergarten. It could tell stories of an elementary-aged girl laughing and gossiping with her friends; a self-conscious junior high girl wondering if everyone could smell the mildew on her clothes; a confident, vivacious teenager holding hands with her boyfriend, praying that he wouldn't realize that she was the one who had passed the foul-smelling gas. The school bus was privy to my childhood and my adolescence, but it was always safe. School buses, like bunk beds, never share the secrets they know; instead they hold them forever within the boundaries of their steel and glass exteriors.

IF ADOLESCENCE IS normally considered a time of disorientation, discovery, and transition, then it is even more so for the adolescent who is living between worlds. It was during adolescence that I vacillated between wanting to be pure American with no question as to my identity, to wanting to be Pakistani. It seemed I was never quite enough of either. When on furlough, I was considered different, but except for the small community in Murree, I was also considered different in Pakistan. I was always too foreign for both places. It was a perpetual roller coaster. Murree, where there were others like me, was my safe place.

But I would find that during those beginning adolescent years that even Murree wasn't safe. Not really.

Those memories begin the summer after I turned eleven, when Mom and I had a car accident. We were going to the school for parent teacher conferences. As an elementary school student I had the day off while my older brothers had gone to school for regular classes. As we headed off in the car, we were fighting. In my pre-pubescent state, I perceived her as the enemy. I don't remember what the fight was about, but I do remember that I was not happy that I had to ride with the enemy to school. I slunk low in the front passenger seat of the car, determined not to make eye contact with the mom-enemy beside me. It was a wet, rainy day during monsoon season, and the road we traveled was slick with mud and rain. Mom saw a can of brake fluid on the bottom of the car, sliding around with every bump and turn. She was distracted. "I have to pick that can up before it slides further," she said.

I was unmoved and barely glanced in her direction, focusing on the can of brake fluid sliding back and forth, coming dangerously close to the gas and brake pedals. In an instant we slid off the road and rolled over the cliff. It was a moment I will never forget.

I was thrown on top of Mom. Her face was pressed against the window on the driver side. The car was precariously perched on its side and when I looked under Mom's head I saw a steep drop. The only thing that seemed to be holding us steady were a few strands of barbed wire. Forest trees surrounded us, and they must have kept us from tumbling over and over down the cliff to a certain death. Mom and I both began to cry.

Suddenly "the enemy" became my dear, sweet, precious mama. How could I have ignored that can of brake fluid, my selfish apathy causing a terrible accident? I did the only thing I knew to do. "Mom, let's pray!" I shouted. I don't even remember what we prayed but we hardly got a word out before we looked up and saw a group of Pakistani men through the windshield and the passenger side window. They were shouting to each other and to us, and we knew that God had answered our barely breathed prayers for rescue. Several of the men held the car steady while the rest of them pulled us out, telling us in Urdu that we would be okay, that they would call for help.

Mom was in great pain and I could tell that something was wrong with her leg. Our neighbors from the cottage where we were making our summer home arrived in record time. Word had reached them that foreigners were in an accident and, having no idea it was us but knowing that in the foreign community there were no strangers, they came running. Mom was taken to the army hospital where skilled doctors x-rayed and cast her leg. The rest of the day is a blur, but I know I was taken back to our home and found out later that I was closely watched for a concussion. The account of the accident made its way through the community quickly, each version told with slight variation. The can of brake fluid morphed into a grapefruit, and our friends wondered how we got grapefruit in Murree when it was clearly out of season. Rumor mixed with truth improved the story each time around.

Much later in life when I saw a picture of Osama bin Laden, I stared at it and wondered why he looked so familiar. It was in a moment of reminiscing that I suddenly realized the man who had pulled me from the overturned car resembled bin Laden. No wonder I always had a difficult time connecting known terror with that picture. On that day so long ago, a bearded Muslim man, a face similar to what would later become the face of terror in western culture, had been our savior and come to our rescue.

Accidents, deformities, tragedies – these were all part of growing up in Pakistan. I never thought to ask why. I don't think the absence of questions indicated fatalism or a callous heart; rather, it was part of life. I knew from early on that there are few things you can control in life, and even those things you think you are able to control will slip out of your fingers in a second and become untouchable.

ALL ADULTS CAN point to a time when they go from the naïveté and simplicity of childhood and cross over into the complicated world of the adult. Some of these coming-of-age moments are dramatic, some are profound. All are life-changing. It is easy to dismiss these moments. They may seem undramatic, insignificant. But to the individual, the drama they represent is a one-way passage out of childhood. Once we pass through we can never go back.

For many years, I would only tell happy stories about my childhood, stories of midnight feasts and camp outs, of traveling to beautiful places and life-long friends. Years went by before I could admit that some of my childhood memories were deeply painful. If I acknowledged just how difficult they were, I would be betraying my parents and my childhood. More than that, if I mentioned the painful parts, I would have to deal with the pain, and some of it went deep.

The real reason I didn't want to tell these stories was more complicated than I wanted to admit. My parents' faith had led them to Pakistan and sustained them through the years they were there. If I was a healthy child, then teenager, then adult, no one could criticize their life choice. Here was their best defense against those critical of the missionary life. If I admitted the pain, if I was truthful about the hard stories, their defense was stripped. But was I really worried about them? Or was I more worried about what would happen to my own faith? If I acknowledged the painful pieces of childhood, could my faith withstand it? Or would I be left with a "where were you God?" echoing hollow in my heart?

A friend of many years, a counselor with a specialty in helping children in trauma, helped me understand the distorted theology that was controlling my memories. When I finally began to admit that all was not perfect, I felt a profound sense of freedom and relief. As I became more honest about my life, I realized the depths of God's care for me and his limitless grace in my journey.

Three events forced me out of the safety of childhood and into a world that was much more difficult to understand.

THE WINTER FOLLOWING the car accident, the year I turned twelve, my parents gave my brothers an air rifle for Christmas. My brothers loved this air rifle. They used it for target shooting, and they learned gun safety. Gun safety was paramount to my non-hunting, non-gun-toting parents. We went on vacation to the city of Shikarpur, and we brought the air rifle along. A friend of mine, just one year older than me, borrowed the gun. He was on the rooftop with a few other children, shooting at birds. Another friend came to the rooftop carrying the infant daughter of a Pakistani couple in her arms. She was chided for bringing the baby to the area. My friend asked her to take the baby down the stairs, off the roof, away from the gun. As he lowered it, the rifle went off. A pellet hit the baby in a soft spot directly behind the ear. She was killed instantly.

The tragedy made no sense at any level.

The following days felt like a terrible dream – a dream that you are unable to wake from, and so you go back to sleep only to relive the terrible dream again. Mom and Dad were two of the first adults that my friend saw after the gun went off. He stood in shock, shaking his head, asking how he would live with this, how he could move forward knowing the baby was dead, knowing a gun in his hands had extinguished a life. Mom's response was clear and authoritative with both challenge and comfort. "You can live with this because of grace. You can live with this because of forgiveness." I was in a back room watching the entire interaction. Her words echo in my memory.

The next day, I went with Mom to the modest two-room house of the baby's parents. Before we even reached the front door, we heard the loud wailing of relatives and friends gathered to express their grief. The baby's mom was not left alone to grieve; instead the community would grieve with her, bear witness to the pain of loss. They would walk her through the difficult days ahead. These things happened in Pakistan – accidents, illness, death – all of these were part of life. You didn't fight them; you walked through them, even as you wailed along the way. But you never walked through them alone. You were surrounded by family and community.

The responses I witnessed to these tragedies were foundational to my faith. The courage of those most affected was profound. No one remained locked in their grief forever. They didn't claim that their pain and suffering were unique or exclusive, though many could have.

The parents of the baby girl were the same. They continued to live. They never pressed charges; they grieved, they wailed, and they moved forward. My friend went on to become a fine physician, one who walked beside others during their grief and loss. We did not talk about the events of that winter for several years, but when we did, it was with mutual understanding of tragedy and loss.

By the following summer, I had stopped talking about this tragedy, although I would often think about it. I have no idea if the adults in our community talked about the death.

To my knowledge, no one ever received counseling for this event. How did people cope? How did those most affected resolve their feelings and their grief? Those are some of the questions that emerged later in my life. At that time, I did not think of or ask those questions. Instead, it was one more chapter in the album of the unexplainable.

Later I would become friends with the mother of the baby girl through my work at the hospital. In my teen years, I would daily see the father during school vacations. Later I would grasp the impact of that day, and I would better understand the fear in the missionary community that there would be retaliation. I would learn of the responses of my parents. But in those days following the accident, I didn't know any of that. I just knew that a baby had tragically died, and that my friend had killed her. Neither of us would ever forget it.

THAT SUMMER *To Sir With Love* came to the cinema in Murree. Films like this were a rare event, and it was an enormous privilege to attend. Several of us were going: my best friend Nancy, some of my brothers and their friends, several I don't remember. We walked together as a large group to a theater located on Murree's long Mall road. The population of Murree tripled in the summer, bringing wealthy Pakistani families for long vacations and those not as wealthy for day trips, and Mall Road held all the main shops and restaurants of a seasonal tourist town.

At thirteen I was fairly well developed. My chest had sprouted breasts, and I had begun to show my inheritance of a curvy round body, the gift of generations of women before me. A young Pakistani man first challenged me with his eyes, and when I quickly looked away reached out his hand and grabbed my buttocks, squeezing as he did so. I felt a mixture of shame and horror. The thought of telling anyone never occurred to me. That's not what we did. We bore the inappropriate touch of men, whether Pakistani or foreign, because we were conditioned to bear it. We now call this sexual harassment, but we had no name for it. It was "no big deal." My innocence challenged, I sat through *To Sir With Love* which held themes of its own that both scared and confused me, themes I didn't understand and wouldn't until later in my teen years.

As girls growing into young women, no one ever talked about being grabbed or touched inappropriately. We all figured this sort of thing happened to everyone, that being touched or treated poorly was just a by-product of being raised as a female in Pakistan. This was not reflective of my life at home, where a father and four brothers were solicitous for my well-being. Nor was it reflective of the men I knew at the church we attended during our school vacations or the Muslim families we visited regularly. This was the behavior of strangers, men and boys who didn't know me and would never see me again, taking liberties that were completely inappropriate. Ironically, if it had been other men or boys touching the women in their families, they would have been justified in violently attacking the man who wronged their women. But I was not one of the women or girls in their family – I was fair game.

The idea that I would acknowledge, much less fight touch, would never have occurred to me. How does that affect a young girl who was becoming a woman? I speak only for myself when I say that it sets a dangerous precedent for suffering shame in silence, for believing I was 'less than,' my body an object instead of an integral part of me as a woman, as a person. In the tapestry that makes up my life, this was one of the pictures woven into the whole. It is a picture that was never discussed, and so I dismissed the feelings, put them aside, telling myself they were unimportant in the bigger tapestry.

There would be other incidents when I was subjected to unwarranted and unwanted looks and touch, where I averted my eyes quickly, my face burning in shame. That day, on the Mall Road in Murree, was the first and it set a pattern of bearing shame in silence. Had I told my mom, the shame and lies might not have penetrated so deeply. I believe we could have talked about it; that talking could have opened up a door into some of her own struggles. But I never mentioned it. I was silent.

I crossed a threshold that night. I entered a world I did not wish to enter and came of age in a way I did not choose. I adhered to the unspoken code of silence that dictated our lives when it came to being touched inappropriately. Through the years the memory would heal. I would learn that God's image is powerful, that though they would try over and over, mere men are no match for those who bear his mark, for those who are called "beloved." God, in his limitless creativity, would find ways to remind me who I was that far outweighed the message that I was an object. Like the story of *The Sound of Music*, wrong and evil may threaten to overpower that which was good, that which was beautiful, but it would never truly win.

IN SOME COMING of age moments, we are spectators; in others, we play the lead role. In sixth grade I became the lead in a drama that threatened to define my entire boarding school experience.

My house parents, Uncle Bill and Aunt Ann, came to Murree with all the confidence of a young, newly-married

American couple who knew everything. They were good-looking, confident, and conservative. We all wanted to be their favorites. They were just that kind of people. Like the popular girl in junior high. You may not trust her, but you want to be her favorite because she is cool and pretty and being her favorite will make you cool and pretty. That was Uncle Bill and Aunt Ann.

The semester had been a rocky one. The beauty of the fall in Murree accompanied by fresh apples of every variety and crisp sunny fall days had given way to a bone-chilling November. We struggled to stay warm in stone buildings that were barely heated with small and smelly kerosene stoves. With the cold came more and more tension in our dormitory. There were eight of us in a room, all pre-teen girls. We fought like feral cats, we gossiped endlessly, we hid our fears and cried into our pillowcases because we were all so miserable.

In November, a gang-like environment had emerged, and I was a gang leader. My rival was a dear friend, who was not dear to me right then. We led rival factions that fought over nothing that I can now remember except Jeff Taylor, the blond and blue-eyed, handsome and suave-as-a-sixth-grader-can-be love interest newly arrived from California by way of Bangladesh. In the summer and early fall he was mine. The unspoken laws of the pre-teen world gave me exclusive rights until I no longer wanted him. He was my boyfriend and I was his girlfriend until death or a pre-teen break-up did us part. But my friend broke the rule. She stole Jeff Taylor from under my nose while I was sick in the infirmary. We divided into rival groups. Susan and her cohort were arrayed against me and my allies, including the formidable Helen, a strong German girl with a mean streak that went deep.

To say Uncle Bill and Aunt Ann were unprepared for their assignment was a gross understatement. The way the children of missionaries were described in Western countries made them sound like mini gods – they may have sinned but not like the general population of children in our passport countries. The kids that Bill and Ann ended up caring for were anything but an angelic host. We were pre-teen girls. We loved the Beatles, mini-skirts, trying on make-up, and Jeff Taylor. We did not take our faith seriously and struggled to find our own place and figure out where we belonged through puberty, boarding school, and our identity as missionary kids who knew little of their passport countries. Our lives changed dramatically between boarding school and 'home' – those places where our parents worked which could be as far away as Sindh, or as close as the capital, a two-hour drive from our school.

We knew our lives were different from the lives of Pakistani young women our age, and we were beginning to be acutely aware of those differences. But we also knew we were different than those in our countries of origin, those countries deemed our places of citizenship through laws written on paper and upheld by governments. By contrast, Bill and Ann were American born and bred. Their first foray into cross-cultural living came in their first four months of marriage. Into this mix came an unrealistic expectation on their part and bad behavior on ours.

At some point Uncle Bill and Auntie Ann cracked. My friend-turned-rival became victim to the first beating. Word spread quickly that she had been beaten with a drumstick. The profound effect on her was apparent, and a level of fear mixed with the cold of that November had all of us wondering who would be next. Somehow, we knew there would be a 'next.'

Helen and I were next. Bill and Ann invited us in, just for a talk, on a Saturday afternoon. They asked us to explain our behavior and admonished us on the many wrongs of that behavior. Uncle Bill held a large Bible, and I'm sure many Bible verses were quoted. I don't remember any of them. I do remember that the phrase "direct disobedience" was used over and over again, and then the dreaded words, "I'm sorry to have to do this to you but if we don't you will never learn...."

I was told to bend over, feet apart. My whole body began to shake as I felt the sting of the twelve-inch drumstick on my backside. Though I knew it had been just a few seconds before, it felt like hours. The lashes kept coming and with them a litany of my sins – "This is for lying," swish, "This is for direct disobedience," swish. Twelve swishes in all. I would have loved to have been stoic, to hold in my tears as an act of ultimate defiance, but I had never felt so much physical pain purposely inflicted by another human being. My tears were for both the physical pain and the awful emotions that accompanied it.

"I'm sorry, please stop!" I kept imploring Bill, but the lashes kept coming. Helen looked on in dread knowing she would be next.

As we tearfully left the apartment, I began counting the hours when I could see Mom's face and be held in her arms. Only two-and-a-half weeks left until the 800-mile journey home. I could not wait.

I was bruised for weeks after the beating, and news of the event spread quickly across the community. It is safe to say that many felt Helen and I were brats and got what was well-deserved. With this, Uncle Bill solidified his place of power, and the punishment was never questioned. I had only one more semester to live under him, and I resolved that the drumstick would never again come down on my backside. Never.

The effect of the beating on our roommates reinforced the fear that already permeated our dorm room. Trust had already eroded. Now the little that was left among us was completely gone. Instead of comforting each other, there were those who used the beatings as threats. "If you don't do such and such, then I'm telling Uncle Bill" really meant "If you don't do whatever I want, then you're going to get the next beating." It was unbearable.

I don't know how Uncle Bill and Aunt Ann communicated to my parents, but I know that before I arrived home, Mom and Dad knew what had happened. Perhaps thinking there could be repercussions, Bill and Ann had penned an articulate, loving letter to my parents. Perhaps it was a boarding report. I don't know. My guess is that it was clothed in language that would absolve them of any guilt over the severity of the punishment, any regret over the way they responded. The "we did this because we love her" and some other carefully worded language would have been a part of this communication. They were able to wound far more with that communication than they had with the drumstick. In my mind, they had influenced my parents before I was able to say a word, before I was able to give my side of the story, as immature as it may have been.

I felt like the comfort that I longed for on that November day and had lived for during the final two weeks of the semester would never come, but, mercifully, the semester ended and I was safely on the train heading home. Vacation had come, the most welcome of any I had ever experienced. With the beating, I had crossed a threshold, I had come of age.

Until that time, I had experienced deep love at times of punishment. I rarely questioned whether I deserved the punishment because there was an undeniable trust of those who punished me. The actions of these boarding parents were actions of an immature couple who had never parented and were in a place where they took their authority too seriously. They saw our normal adolescent behavior, if not stopped, as evidence of rebellion in the future that would have eternal consequences. Intuitively I knew that the punishment did not fit the offense. I knew that the punishment was too severe, that they had overstepped a boundary that should not have been crossed.

In communicating with my parents, Uncle Bill had given me the thirteenth lash. He had reached them, and gained their trust, before I could say a word, and it seemed more than I could live with. But sheltered in the walls of my home, present with those that loved me even when they didn't know my heart's pain, I healed. The power of grace and forgiveness in my life was far more powerful than the sting of a drumstick, the healing of God more lasting than the actions of an immature adult.

I learned that some pain cannot be measured. As I went on to become a nurse, I knew instinctively that though the Western world tries hard to measure pain with their linear scales and numbers, some pain is so deep that a number can never express its affect or impact. It's into this pain that the Spirit of God alone speaks. It's he who whispers, "I am with you, you are not alone." He who whispers the word "beloved," and though the shouting pain threatens to drown out the voice, the whisper is as powerful as a well-equipped army, as strong as the strongest of pain medications.

That winter, God's whispers healed me, and though afraid to go back to boarding school in the spring, I knew I could do it. There was no thirteenth lash. The punishment didn't win. Love and grace were infinitely stronger than the beating of a drumstick.

❖

THE DRUMSTICK BEATING did nothing to improve my behavior, or correct my "direct disobedience." In fact, I grew far worse. My thirteen-year-old self was insufferable. While many people know this in the abstract from memories, I have proof in the form of a bright red diary – kept sporadically throughout the year from 1973 to 1974. Little did I know that events in Pakistan were shaping history and I would live to regret my egocentric thirteen-year-old self.

The diary is hilarious and pathetic, giving the reader a window into how much my life resembled a typical American teenager. Boys and girlfriends fill up a majority of the pages. There are references to fights between my mother and me, sibling love and squabbles, and trips to boarding school, Karachi, and other local places. Pages are written with my name plus the boy who was flavor of the month. "Marilyn and Tom forever." "Marilyn and Phil Forever." "Tom loves Marilyn." "Phil loves Marilyn." "Marilyn loves Phil." Here I was, in a land that I've missed every day since I left it, and all I could write about is boys and adolescent heartache. I would rewrite the words to Christian songs, removing the names Jesus and God and putting in the names of my current beau. In fairness to my teenage brain, this says as much about the shallow theology of the songs as it does about the brain of an adolescent.

Occasionally the diary shows a spark of empathy – at the death of a friend's father, at the near death of my Pakistani girlfriend, Angel – but overall its interest to me is in its normalcy. This is the fascinating thing about a life between worlds. It is at points as normal as any thirteen-year-old growing up in their passport country and at other times could no more resemble "normal" than a man walking on air.

The diary also tells a story of faith that oscillates through its pages. One day I am a Christian and want to please God; the next day I am angry with the world and particularly cross at God. One entry tells a story of a teenager with her mind on eternity and a sensitivity to the spiritual, the next discards all that with the stroke of a pen, writing instead about boys and cigarettes, about getting in trouble with house parents and annoying parents.

Grades 7 and 8 found me ready to try anything that was off limits. K-2 unfiltered cigarettes found their way from the local vendor to the perfect spot under my mattress, where I hid them until other friends could come over and enjoy the excitement of forbidden, if ghastly-tasting, fruit. These were so terrible that they were an excellent public health intervention, guaranteed to turn a teenager away from smoking quickly and forever. The marijuana that grew behind Holy Trinity Church in Murree was also a hidden offense, though none of us knew how to use it properly. It held little appeal other than being off limits. A bigger problem was the ease of buying illicit drugs over the counter. These were guaranteed to give you a high, then a low, and, if caught, suspension from school. We used them with no knowledge of their potency and a dangerous belief in our immortality. That I was saved from myself is clear, and I shudder to think of what could have been the outcome of my actions. The same strength that was a gift in surviving and thriving in boarding school was a weakness when it manifested itself in the strong will of a young teenager bent on breaking rules.

The summer after I turned thirteen a few of us got into everything there was to get into. We were in junior high and didn't have the sense to recognize that all things should not be experienced. Had we been children of diplomats and caught using the drugs we were using, it would have been the end of our parents' diplomatic careers. The missionary community was more forgiving. I learned just how forgiving when I made a visit back to Pakistan just before my senior year of nursing school. I was invited to dinner at the apartment of the boarding administrator, Marge Montgomery. Marge and her sister Rosie Stewart were fixtures at the school. With their kindly smiles and set ways, Marge made sure bills were paid, schedules made, and boarding staff happy. Rosie was the piano teacher, teaching chubby and clumsy fingers to play Chopin's Polonaise in A and Beethoven's Für Elise, occasionally discovering real talent among us. Auntie Rosie's patience with non-practicing, untalented children was legendary.

As I sat in their home at the age of twenty, full of life and energy, articulate about God's role in my world, Rosie shook her head in amazement and said to me and Marge with wonder, "Isn't it amazing how some of the worst kids turned out the best?!" It wasn't until that moment that I was truly aware of how far I had come and how much trouble I had given my parents, my boarding staff, and my teachers.

ADDED TO THE discomfort of my junior high years was the ever-present competition in sports. Murree was not kind to unathletic children. Sports played a big role in the school community in determining "popularity potential." In the fall, when leaves were changing from green to gold there was field hockey for the girls and flag football for the guys. As November came, and the cold, stone classrooms held the smell of kerosene from tiny heaters that worked overtime to offer at least a bit of heat, athletes kept warm on the sports fields playing soccer. And in the spring, there were basketball teams for both girls and boys.

As far back as I can remember, whether the game was Capture the Flag or Steal the Bacon, I was last to be picked for any team. When I was little it was tolerable, but as I entered into junior high, I dreaded standing in line and waiting… waiting… waiting as girls and boys were one by one picked to join a team. It inevitably came down to one or two of us and the silent prayer, "Please God, let them pick me, don't let me be last, not this time God…" The older I got, the more I realized there were probably competing prayers prayed in those dreadful moments, and I wondered how God decided the outcome.

Was it like picking a daisy and pulling off the petals the way a preteen decides whether the boy in question "loves me or loves me not?" Was it all about picking the winning petal?

Sometimes my prayer was answered. Other times the person standing with me was picked, and I could hear the audible sigh the minute her name was called. I dared not glance up to see her look of pity as she awkwardly ran to take her place. It is easy to write and laugh about this now. No matter how good anyone at Murree was at sports, none went on to compete professionally; they were good, but they weren't that good. Their achievements were limited to our small school "nestled 'neath the great Himalayas." Faded black-and-white photos showing teams lined up in crisp uniforms are all that's left of their athletic prowess.

I once made it onto the girls' soccer team. In my junior year of high school the Walsh girls were unable to attend an inter-school tournament at the end of the semester. Sheryl and Shelley Walsh lived in Bangladesh, and they had already booked flights back home. The Walsh twins were a reminder that life is not fair. They were beautiful, smart, kind, and athletic. They captured the imagination of every boy at Murree and the envy of many of us girls. That year, I got to take their place on the soccer field and go to the tournament. I played my hardest but, by all accounts, the trade was unfair.

The inability to cross the athletic line, a line that held such prestige at my school, brought much pain and adolescent angst. I learned later that many of us had deep feelings of insecurity in these areas, all unspoken for fear we were the only ones. With so much else to worry about – friendships, life in dormitories, homesickness, coping with competing cultures of boarding school, home, our passport countries, and our adopted country – athletic angst only rose to the surface during those days when we had gym class. Otherwise, the feelings were suppressed into backspaces of the mind and memory, coming out through rueful laughter in later years.

MY BRIGHT RED diary tells of a faith that ebbed and flowed through the shifting hormones of adolescence. One week I write, "I can never be a Christian. It's all fake." The next week I write, "I know I want to follow God. It's just really hard sometimes." The ups and downs of my faith were correlated with whether the current boy I liked liked me back, or whether my best friend and I were fighting or not. In truth, faith had been such a constant part of my life that it was impossible to think of it as something separate and abstract. It was like the faith of the Muslims that surrounded me – a way of life as opposed to a separate entity. You didn't separate your faith from all of life.

Faith in my younger years consisted of nightly devotions and praying for our parents far away from our boarding school, doing "God's work." Funny that my parents never put their work that way. It was boarding school that attached "God" to the "work," not Mom and Dad. Maybe that's why their faith became winsome to me instead of joyless and legalistic.

Faith was weekly Friday chapel services bringing in speakers and singing. Faith was Sunday morning church held in our large school auditorium during the school year, in small Pakistani churches during our school vacations, and in Holy Trinity Church, the large and noble church built by the British in the 1800s in the town of Murree during summers. Faith was Baptist singspirations as a child and Sunday night singspirations in junior high.

Old hymns still echo through my mind:

There is power, power, wonder-working power,
In the blood (in the blood) of the lamb (of the lamb).

Marvelous grace of our loving Lord,

Mercy there was great and grace was free.
Pardon there was multiplied for me,
there my burdened soul found liberty, at Calvary.

These were the songs sung by missionaries gathered together in the summer twilight. They lived in a country that alternated between hospitable and hostile, and they lived a life far removed from the churches and families they loved. These times were times that revived their souls and brought comfort in this land they loved and served in the best way they knew how. It was these songs that soaked into the marrow of their children, many of whom would go on to leave their Baptist roots but hold dear their parents and the foundation of their adult faith.

In those younger years, I knew surely and simply that I loved God. And I knew that He loved me. There were no questions. There were no whys. There was God and there was Me. We two were on a journey. Later, when the whys and the questions came, I would cry out in pain over betrayal and in agony over the unfairness of life. But faith in the early years was simple and solid, heard from my parents, echoed in my school, rooted in my life. It was not complicated by what-ifs and whys.

The climate where this faith flourished was in a missionary sub-culture. But the outside world echoed with faith as well. There were no atheists. God was alive and well. Whether in the mosque or the church, he existed, and he ordered the lives of those around us. Whether you were Muslim or Christian, faith was a way of life, not an appendage.

Long before I ever heard church bells ringing, the call to prayer had rooted its way into my conscious and subconscious mind. I cannot remember a time when I didn't love the call to prayer that echoed across cities, towns, and villages five times a day. I didn't even know what the words meant until I was in high school, but they brought comfort and security. As soon as I heard the call to prayer, I knew I was home. The call to prayer ordered our day from sunup to sundown. I never found this incongruous to our Christian faith. I overheard my mother telling a Muslim friend one day, when asked when she prayed, that she woke up at the first *azzan* and prayed then and through the day.

It was true. I could never wake up earlier than my parents. They were awake at the first *azzan*, partaking of their bread of life. This was their sustenance, their life-blood, what gave them purpose and reason for being miles away from family and all that was familiar.

Early on, I have memories of Dad taking us kids to large mosques in the city of Hyderabad during Eid celebrations. I was eyewitness to thousands of faithful Muslims gathered at the mosque to pray in unison, each movement, from standing to kneeling, full of meaning and reverence. In public, we witnessed only men praying; women in this area stayed home and did their prayers. Indeed, if we visited someone's home and the *azzan* was heard, women, particularly the elderly, would excuse themselves to go and pray. Mom and I would cover our heads with our *dupattas* during this time out of respect for the faith of our Muslim friends.

So either I chose faith or faith chose me – as a child, it was impossible to know. If there was ever a time when I wanted to throw my faith away, it was during the year when the baby died and I got beaten by a drumstick. That was the closest I came in childhood to tossing it off the Murree hillside, watching it go to the bottom of a rocky crevice in the mountains where it would surely die, like all the people in the buses that would go over these cliffs. The death of the baby, betrayal and beating by a houseparent, and the inappropriate touch of a young man were all events that built up, and I can trace the words in my diary to those specific events. Though I never wrote about the events themselves, the ups and downs of my faith journey tell the story.

But my faith didn't die. Instead it grew in the shadows, continuing to emerge in unlikely moments, surprising both me and others with its tenacity.

CHAPTER 5
FLYING HOME

Harry kicked off hard from the ground. The cool night air rushed through his hair as the neat square gardens of Privet Drive fell away…. He felt as though his heart was going to explode with pleasure; he was flying again, flying away from Privet Drive as he'd been fantasizing about all summer, he was going home…. For a few glorious moments, all his problems seemed to recede into nothing, insignificant in the vast, starry sky.

JK Rowling, *Harry Potter and the Order of the Phoenix*

I LOVE AIRPLANES. From the cardboard meals eaten in tight quarters, to the extreme fatigue as you make your way to the tiny bathroom at the end of a long transnational flight, I love flying and everything that goes along with it. Planes and travel make me feel alive, humble me, and bring indescribable excitement. I become like a little girl.

The story of how the Wright brothers changed the world forever is well-known. Not so well-known is how flying became affordable for the average person, including our family. In 1914 a "seaplane" began service across Tampa Bay, but commercial flying was not embraced quickly. During World War I, aircraft were associated with military operations, not transportation. The advent of "air mail" in 1917 changed this when the United States government began using planes for mail, and "via airmail" was stamped across envelopes throughout the country. Then in 1969 Pan Am, short for Pan American Airlines, the unofficial U.S. flag carrier, inaugurated the Boeing 747, a massive four-engine aircraft that could carry as many as 450 people and was twice as big as any other jet. The 747 would become an iconic part of my experience.

In my early childhood, it was customary to dress up when flying. Just as Mom had worn pearls and a sophisticated suit when boarding ships in her early years of travel, we put on our best clothes to fly around the world. I still have an aversion to traveling in sweat pants.

These major transatlantic or transpacific flights happened every four years, but when they came, my parents made the most of them. We never travelled straight back to the United States. We always took the long route, stopping in Bangkok, Hong Kong, Japan, and Hawaii when we went the West Coast route, or various countries in Europe or the United Kingdom when we went the east coast route. Either way, by the time I left home I had been in more countries than I could count, had eaten brioche with strong coffee in small *pension*s in Austria, had milked goats in Germany, and had shopped for electronics in Hong Kong. I had also seen major cathedrals, mosques, and landmarks in every country we visited. The richness of these experiences was often lost on me. It was a normal part of our lives, and I did not yet fully appreciate how vast and amazing our world is, how tiny we are in comparison.

My romance with flying began with furloughs. I thought I loved furloughs, although, in reality, before we returned to the United States in 1974, I had experienced only two, one when I was four going on five, the other when I was nine going on ten. I liked the flying to and from, the shopping, the food. I loved relatives, and Christmases with Grandma K, aunts, uncles, and cousins. I liked that I was different, special. But in the summer of 1974, when we began a year-long furlough that would stretch into two, I was fourteen, an age of dramatic, day-to-day changes. One day I was the most secure adolescent found anywhere on the globe, in any country or culture; the next day I was a crying mess of emotions who fit in nowhere, least of all my passport country.

Stan graduated from high school that summer, and the day after graduation Mom, Dad, my younger brother Danny, my cousin Barbara, and I headed off on a weeklong journey to the United States via Pakistan International Airlines. In Vienna, we stayed at a *pension*, eating brioche and drinking strong coffee each morning, and visited the famed Lipizzaner stallions. In Germany, we stayed with a delightful German family on acres of beautiful farmland, visiting Koln and Frankfurt along the way. We were treated with food and hospitality, and welcomed as part of the family. It was on this trip that I milked a goat, discovered that I didn't like warm

milk straight from the source, and learned my only German –
Mein auto ist kaput! (My car is broken!). I also tasted my first
liqueur-filled chocolate, which, for a missionary kid who had
never tasted alcohol, felt scandalous. I ate more than a few
chocolates that day, feeling sweetly devious and grown-up. In
Zurich we stayed just streets away from the family of a boy in
my class, my first true love, and traveled with his family into
the Alps via a cog railway.

Meanwhile, my brothers were having adventures
more dangerous than milking goats and drinking liqueur-
filled chocolates. Stan and Tom headed overland through
Afghanistan, Iran, and Turkey, planning to arrive over a
month later. In the 1970s, this overland route was well-
travelled, and boys who grew up at Murree had a strong
sense of adventure, knew how to travel independently, and
needed few luxuries. The excitement was in the journey.

My own journey ended at Logan International Airport
in Boston, where a large crowd had gathered to meet us with
Ed and his fiancée, Sharon, at the front. We were nervously
excited about meeting Sharon. She would be the first addition
to our family through marriage, and we were anticipating a
large wedding on the campus of Gordon College in August.

The trip back to the United States and the summer of
family fun held no hint that the two years ahead would be
some of my most difficult. In Pakistan I identified as an
American. I wanted miniskirts and rock music and took an
increasingly superior attitude towards my Pakistani friends.
I was at times completely unbearable. I may have been a
missionary kid, but I was the one of the superior boarding
school education and air travel to America every fifth year.
Everything changed that furlough.

I began grade 9 in Winchendon in the fall of 1974. To say
I was scared is a disservice to my adolescent emotions. I was

terrified. My older cousins lived next door, but I was still the little cousin without status or popularity. My currency had not been established. Two weeks before school began, my brother Tom headed off to football camp. After we visited him I began to dread what was coming. He looked miserable, and something inside of me died for him. How bad was it? He was a senior in high school, away from all he knew and loved. He was away from his best friend, his classmates that he had grown up with, his beloved Murree, and away from teachers who admired and respected his brain. He would have to forge his way in a new, alien world in an impossibly short span of time. I left that visit with an inexpressible dread in my heart; I felt that I would soon experience hell.

While visiting Tom at football camp I decided Jesus needed to return before I began high school in an American public school. There was no way Jesus would make me go through that sort of agony and terror. I began to pray. The movie *A Thief in the Night* was released that year, telling the story of the end of the world and those left behind on earth because of their unbelief. I had already memorized the song "I Wish We'd All Been Ready," a lament for those who would miss the rapture only to be left behind at horrible football camps and in American public high schools. I knew *I* was ready, and that was all that mattered. I didn't care if the rest of the world went to hell, I just knew that hell for me was starting school and if Jesus was worth anything he'd better show up. I shared this with Stan just two days before school started. He looked at me confidently and said, "He won't come back; he wants you to go through this." Such callousness offended me; I vowed not to speak to him for some time.

Early on a September morning just after Labor Day, I headed off to school. My memories of the day are fuzzy.

At the large double doors to the school I heard words that I had never heard spoken aloud before. Words like these had sometimes been whispered in the hallowed halls of my Christian boarding school, but this was a full assault on my tender, virgin ears. I was shoved aside as I tried to make my way into the crowded halls.

The morning was a blur. I found my way to homeroom and realized I didn't know the words to the American Pledge of Allegiance. The class stood together and faced the flag. My eyes darted to my left and to my right to see what my classmates were doing. We were in alphabetical order, and I would soon learn that Brenda Botti was on my left and Steve Carter was on my right. Both would soon become good friends, but right then they were scary strangers, far more confident than me. Both were looking at the flag and had their right hands placed across their chests. I nervously did the same. An adult voice was broadcast through a scratchy intercom and the words began:

"I pledge allegiance to the flag of the United States of America...." All the mouths surrounding me were uttering the same words. Red-faced, I began murmuring something. I don't know what it was, but it wasn't the pledge of allegiance. The pledge, which normally takes barely a minute, seemed to last for a lifetime. A lifetime of insecurity. A lifetime of not belonging. My heart beat so fast that I was sure people could hear it. I was uncomfortable in my clothes – clothes that had seemed fine that morning but suddenly felt tight and ill-fitting. My face was red and my mouth was dry with nervous emotion. Finally, the pledge ended and chairs scraped along the floor as people sat down.

This scenario would be repeated for my own children when we moved to the United States from Cairo, Egypt, many years later. My middle son would write, "I knew about flags, but I didn't know about allegiance." So it was with me. On my fifteen-year-old stage, this was my opening act and I felt small and insignificant, insecurity flooding over me in waves. My ears burned as I assumed everyone around me was talking about me. It wasn't just paranoia. It was a small town that didn't see many new kids. They *were* talking about me. I was late to every class and ready to cry by ten in the morning.

In third period science class I met someone who I was convinced would make my life miserable for the rest of the year, maybe even the rest of my life. The girl sitting behind me was my exact opposite – sophisticated, pretty, and, above all, thin. Looking at her was enough to make me believe in the Greek gods – capricious, malicious, and gorgeous. She was everything that I was not. The mean girl seemed to take an instant dislike to me, slowly eyeing me, top to bottom. She ended her critical survey with my toes, which were brightly painted with shiny red polish. No one in 1970s New England wore toenail polish, least of all someone in grade 9. She stared. Then she turned to her friend, the girl beside her, to discuss this strange alien creature who had entered their classroom.

I couldn't wait to get home. *This* was America. This place – this cold, chaotic, small-minded place where the natives laughed at a teenager with red toenail polish – represented what was known on the world stage as the greatest country on the globe. This was a jungle. Years later the movie *Mean Girls* told the story of a teenager who moved to the United States from Africa where she had lived with her anthropologist parents. The movie portrayed the teenage world in the United States as a world of wild beasts – tigers, lions, and laughing hyenas – disguised as teenagers. My first day at an American high school felt like that.

I missed my small school in Pakistan so much that it hurt. Boarding school may have been hard, but this was impossible. I would not go back to the jungle the next day. I couldn't go back. And where on earth was Jesus? I had asked so little of him. He was proving completely untrustworthy, and I would have none of it. I went to bed heavy of heart and angry at Jesus. It was a bad mixture.

Mom's insistent voice was my alarm clock the next morning, and I knew there was no way around this fire. I had to walk through it, regardless of the burns I would sustain. For three days I suffered. Then on day four my fate suddenly changed. The pretty, sophisticated, thin girl talked to me. When I shuffled into science class, eyes on the ground, defeated as only a fourteen year-old can be defeated, the beautiful, blonde, mean girl caught my eyes and said: "Hey you! You were my best friend in Miss Crowley's four-year-old kindergarten!"

"I was?" I said with a small voice.

"Yes." After day three of terrorizing me, she went home and told her mom about the interaction. Her mom looked at her and said, "Marilyn? Marilyn Brown? She was your best friend in kindergarten!"

Her name was Christie and in that science class, a life-long friendship began. Christie is still sophisticated, thin, and beautiful, but after those initial days of terror and intimidation, it all changed. Behind that face was someone who could laugh and have fun, who was loyal to the bone, who loved and welcomed me.

My time in Winchendon extended from grade 9 and into grade 10. I became a varsity cheerleader and a carnival queen for my class. I smoked pot. I tasted beer. I was a third culture missionary kid trying to make sense of the world around me in whatever way I could. But furlough was not for me. I was to go back to Pakistan in the July before grade 11 and shake the dust of a public American high school off feet that were still adorned with their bright red toe nail polish. I would go back to *tongas*, buses, and trains; my passage through Pakistan would continue. I could not have been happier.

VISITING CHURCHES WAS mandatory for the missionary on furlough. My parents were determined to keep as much of a sense of consistency and normalcy as possible during these year-long furloughs, so they carefully decided when and where we would go as a family, and when and where my father would visit churches alone. This was critically important to our family, and I am grateful for their wisdom.

In Pakistan we were often a novelty. As a little white missionary kid, and later an older white missionary kid, I was stared at constantly. I had no color. I looked different from all those around. I sometimes hated the attention, hated being stared at, wanted to lash out at those who stared, to mock them. Other times, I welcomed the attention. It made me feel special. It made me feel superior to those around me.

In Pakistan I was set apart as a privileged little white girl. On home leave, visiting small New England churches, I was also different. And being stared at in churches by American villagers turned out to be far worse than being stared at by Pakistani villagers. Rural Pakistani children gawked at us out of curiosity; at youth groups in New England we faced equally curious stares, but I found them harsher. This was the place I was supposed to belong, this was the place where my parents had been born and raised. Mom and Dad called New England "home" so, in my reasoning, it should have been easier. But it wasn't. Instead, attending strange Sunday School classes or youth groups in New England was like being paraded as a new animal in a zoo. My face burned at the audible whispers.

"Are they missionary kids?"

"I don't know."

"Look at her red toes."

Once again, the red toes had given me away. Oh why, why hadn't I learned the first time? Thankfully, winter would soon be upon us, and my red toes would soon be hidden in thick boots and socks.

I had learned how to work with stares and attention in Pakistan. I had learned how to discern when the stares were rude and demanded response, and when they were just curious. I knew what to say and how to live. But I had no idea how to respond to Christian youth groups in the United States. My favorite visit was to a church in New Hampshire, where a girl took me under her wing. She treated me like I was completely normal, took me to a store, and taught me how to shoplift. She left me with the best memory I have of visiting a church.

Small town New England in the 1970s was largely Catholic. I didn't know then that the kids in these youth groups were facing their own struggles of being Protestant in a Catholic area. Even if their ancestors had come on "the Boat" (the vernacular for the Mayflower), they still faced battles to belong. When you're a teenager, your own ego goes into protective mode, and what better way to protect myself than to be arrogant and dismissive. If I dismissed them, then I was in control. Far better that than have them dismiss me.

At the Bethany Bible Chapel in Winchendon, I had good friends. Melanie Epps had reached out to me in the first few days of arrival. Bruce Beckwith was a friend and a crush. Gail, Marylou, and others had become friends and confidantes. The Chapel youth group had grown exponentially when my brother Tom and I arrived. Kids found out that we were there on Sundays, so they came on Sundays. We went apple picking and had game nights; went hiking in the fall and occasionally attended sports games together. Largely it was a social group, and I don't remember leaning on it for any sort of spiritual guidance. That could be because I wasn't looking for spiritual guidance. I was merely trying to find a place to belong.

Outwardly I made friends and I was popular and involved. Inwardly I was aching. I ached with longing for the old church building that housed our Murree classrooms, that froze in the winter and echoed with the sound of monsoon rains in the summer. I ached for familiar people and faces, for those who had known me since birth. I had experienced many times of homesickness in the past – but that was within Pakistan. This was different. I was experiencing the first of many episodes of geographic longing. It was also my first experience of recognizing the giant chasm between worlds, a chasm separated by more than an ocean. It was a chasm of culture and food and people and faith, and I was suspended somewhere in the middle of the chasm.

I did not know how to live in America. I was forever a foreigner in a place where I thought I should feel more at home. My parents did not know how to parent in America. They were unprepared for the challenges of homecoming dances, dating, boyfriends, class rings, and cheerleading. This was a new journey for all of us. My parents had launched two of their children: Ed was married and finishing up college ,and Stan was in college. Tom was a senior in high school, navigating his own tough waters and away from all that he knew and loved. Dan was still in elementary school. I, meanwhile, was oblivious. And I was not an easy teenager. My tongue often ran away without my brain, and I never worried about consequences. I had somehow survived that first day of American high school, but that year and the following one became years of angst and rebellion.

I NEVER BECAME used to visiting strange churches that supported our family. Theoretically I was supposed to belong in these churches. Weren't my parents part of this? And by default, shouldn't I have been part?

Another factor was at play here. These were the churches that gave money so that my parents could be in Pakistan. They were not anonymous buildings or faceless people; they were part of what my parents called the "Body of Christ." I didn't really know what that meant. This was a body, I had been taught, in which people care for one another in tangible, practical ways. This meant more than bringing finger sandwiches and lemonade to funerals and making quilts at missionary circles; it was supposed to mean caring for people beyond your comfort level. This was supposed to be a group of people that supported and believed in what my parents were doing in Pakistan. My parents had talked about the many ways they had been loved by this group of people, but in my current adolescent state, I couldn't hear it.

A few years ago, in an attempt to capture my feelings and memories of this group, I wrote an imaginary letter to these supporting churches:

> *You tried so hard!*
>
> *You went through your children's clothes, certain that you could find something, anything really, that you could send to the children of missionaries. You pictured the huts we lived in, the threadbare tunics we wore, the lack of*

stores and supplies. You thought we would never know the difference between Levis and no name jeans.

You advertised and arranged special drop off times so those clothes could make their way from your basements to our homes, our bodies.

You packed up oatmeal, and flour, thinking that surely we would use these products and be so excited when they arrived. It never entered your mind that chocolate chips and taco mix were what we craved.

You really did send tea bags to the part of the world that invented tea.

You sent pants with no zippers and old-fashioned dresses, all with love and a pure heart. And we mocked with hearts that were mean and not pure.

And I thought you were well-meaning and clueless. And I laughed.

And then I began meeting some of you. And you really didn't know. You really were giving us gifts from your heart. You were taking time and energy that could have been used in a hundred other ways to care for us so far away.

You put little stitches on big warm quilts and sent them our way so we could be warm. And with each stitch you prayed for us. You prayed. And prayed. And prayed.

When my mother and I went over a cliff in the mountains, with only a barbed wire fence separating us from certain death – you were praying. When my brother got in a near-fatal accident in Turkey, you were praying. When we faced illness, and sorrow, and separation, you prayed. When babies died, and boarding school was too hard, and people hurt us, you prayed.

You were so much better than me – with my arrogance and my "well-meaning but clueless" song and dance. You prayed with a fervor and love that I never had. You knew what it was to care for people you had barely met.

I still have two of your quilts. And when I look at them I think of how much I judged – and how wrong I was. And I thank you in my heart.

My response to New England churches and youth groups was the beginning of my disconnect from "American Christianity." This disconnect has haunted me, and I have vacillated between guilt, anger, and resignation. I could accept cultural differences in other places. But legally and spiritually I was *supposed* to belong in the United States, and especially in American Evangelical communities of faith. They were *supposed* to be safe, but in my mind, they had failed. So I never allowed myself to fully enter these communities. I was unable to shake off the experiences of my youth. I remained the 'animal in a zoo' well into my adulthood. I would finally find my home within Eastern Orthodoxy, an ancient faith that has survived centuries, passed down through icons, the church fathers, and the Scriptures.

But that would be a much later chapter in my story.

As the two-year furlough came to an end, I couldn't wait to get back to Pakistan. The thin blue aerogrammes again flew back and forth between Pakistan and Winchendon, my soul poured out to my friends back in Pakistan. I tried to make it seem like all was wonderful, stories that told of a popular, cute, cheerleader who had adjusted beautifully. And in a way I had. I had many friends. Everyone knew the girl from Pakistan. I was an enigma in this small town that lived under the shadow of a giant rocking horse.

If one story captures all of the angst and discomfort of my teenage years in the United States it is the story of how I became "Carnival Queen." I was in Grade 9 and it was winter. The high school had an annual winter carnival that included snow sculptures, special events, a bonfire, and a grand finale in the form of a winter dance. Every grade was allowed to pick a "queen" who would then go on to compete with other nominees. She would be crowned during the winter dance, to the envy of all her friends. I was picked to be the Carnival Queen in our class. It was a bit like Prom Queen. I have a feeling that two of my guy friends filled in extra ballots to be sure that I won, but the way I won didn't matter. The fact is that I, a nobody little missionary kid from Pakistan, was picked to be Carnival Queen.

There was only one problem: I was not allowed to date, and I most certainly was not allowed to go to school dances. I was in a dilemma. I was convinced that my parents would see the value of this nomination and relax the house rules for just one night, but alas – it was not to be. Dad was traveling and Mom was solo parenting – the decision was final. I would not go to the dance. I would not be crowned Carnival Queen of the whole school.

Or would I? My ability to deceive was not just limited to hiding novels under the bedclothes. Come the proverbial hell or high water, I would be at that dance. I went off to youth group that night, sullen and angry, but determined. At the appointed time, my friend showed up to youth group and picked me up, and we went to that dance. It was a terrible time. A guilty conscience combined with being the only Carnival Queen who was not in a formal gown proved to be a miserable mix. I did not win the school nomination. I snuck home heavy of heart, angry at my parents, and angry at the entire student body of the high school. I fell into an anxious sleep, dreaming of the comfort of my school setting in Pakistan, where Carnival Queens and school dances were nonexistent and where I was the princess of quite a lot without even trying.

Added to the social discomfort was the fact that I did not like myself. I was uncomfortable in my skin. Besides having a constant inner ache, I became fat, a closet eater. I pilfered food from the refrigerator and stole leftovers from dinner plates. I gained thirty pounds, and every pound showed on my five-foot, three-inch frame. I counted the days until I would leave, and I grew fatter. Like Eustace in C.S Lewis's *Voyage of the Dawn Treader,* I was self-centered, proud, and whined about everything. And just as Eustace became on the outside what he already was on the inside, his body transformed into a huge, scaly dragon, so too my internal reality shaped what I was on the outside.

For Eustace the story did not end there, and neither would it for me. Eustace was transformed back to a boy through the work of Aslan and became a different person. He was stripped. Layers and layers of dragon skin were peeled away until his soft, boy skin was once again revealed:

> "*The very first tear he made was so deep that I thought it had gone right into my heart. And when he began pulling the skin off, it hurt worse than anything I've ever felt. The only thing that made me able to bear it was just the pleasure of feeling the stuff peel off.*"

When I look back, I don't always want to remember those years. I prefer to remember what it was like when I was able to feel myself transformed, when I would have the *"pleasure of feeling the stuff peel off."*

But furloughs are a part of the whole, a big piece of the story lived between two worlds. I didn't transform in the United States. It never seemed possible. It was in Pakistan that I could transform, from caterpillar to butterfly, from dragon to girl, from self-centered and miserable with ill-fitting skin to open and willing to learn, comfortable with who I was. So I grew up and I grew fat. And I counted the days until I would return to the security of Pakistan.

In Pakistan, we were part of a community. Though imperfect and flawed, we shared all of life together in a place where we were all foreigners. We were deeply close, connected in a way that goes well beyond normal neighborhood relationships. We were part of a small group that lived counter-culture in both our adopted country and our passport countries. We lived apart from blood relatives, and so those around us became relatives in proxy. We inherited each other's houses, cars, clothes, families, and dolls. So it would be easy to leave blood relatives and my life in the United States. Pakistan was my home – the place where I belonged.

So I remained an awkward, overweight teenager, desperate to figure out who and what I was. I did not find hope for my identity in the churches that gave sacrificially to our family. I did not find it in the youth groups – groups that were minorities in their own right in the midst of Catholic New England. And I did not find it in popularity and activity at Winchendon's Murdock High School. I found it when I returned home to Pakistan. I knew that I didn't want to live like I had for those two years. I was sick of being fat. I was sick of trying so hard to be popular. I was sick of not belonging. I was desperate for home. I was sick of life being all about me.

When we left Winchendon on our journey back to Pakistan by way of California, I breathed an exultant sigh of relief.

WHEN I WALKED off the plane onto Pakistani soil, a burden lifted. I could begin again. I could leave the past two years behind. In the United States my faith went into a holding pattern, unable to be fully born until I returned to a place of security and belonging. Here the extra weight I carried from two years of poor eating and insecurity could be shed, along with my Eustace Scrubb skin. The cut would be deep, but oh, so freeing.

Perhaps that is why I remember my junior and senior years of school with such fondness. I continued to invite punishment for breaking rules, smoking, and boy problems. But these were years of growth and contentment in my inner core. I came away with a tremendous self-confidence that still surprises me given who I had been the two years before.

I arrived back fat. Mom will probably chide me as she reads this and claim that I was not fat. Indeed, some cousins at the time consoled me by saying, "You're not fat, you're just fluffy!" But I knew differently. I had become a big girl. A pretty face was overshadowed by large thighs and big breasts. Being big came from heredity accompanied by a large side-dish of hotdogs, burgers, and ice cream – too much food and too little exercise. People described me the way fat girls have been described through the ages. "She has such a pretty face!" Other phrases were unspoken. "She's fat. What's wrong with her? She must not exercise enough. Why doesn't she lose weight?"

At Murree, no one could ever be fat. Horrible food, a lot of walking, and regular cases of pinworms produced a population of children that did not struggle with weight. I was the exception. Genes had blessed me with a healthy appetite and tendency toward plumpness, and it became one of the pains of my childhood. Being called "fatty" was the ultimate insult. The sting of those words from my brother's friends has stayed with me through the years, even after I arrived and stayed at a normal weight for a long time. But nasty people will get their comeuppance. I peruse pictures of these men who called me fatty, now bald and middle-aged and unable to hold in bellies that once were muscular and young. "Who looks better now?" I want to shout. Instead, I laugh silently, aware that the sting of name-calling in adolescence fades, but never really goes away.

When I arrived back in Pakistan from the U.S. in 1976, I knew instinctively that when I began walking the high hills of Murree I would take off weight, and take off weight I did. Although the chubby image remained etched in my mind, before long I had shed pounds and inches. But it was about far more than weight loss. It was about belonging. I was back where I belonged. I had spent two years trying so hard, trying to fit, trying to say and do the right things.

And now I was back. I no longer had a frenzied desire to fit in. I was back with my tribe and I belonged. Belonging had never tasted so sweet. My attitude toward Pakistan would also change during these years. The sense of curiosity and empathy for my adopted culture that was developing in my younger years grew exponentially. I wore exclusively Pakistani clothes and tried to learn more about Pakistan. While volunteering at Shikarpur Christian Hospital during winter vacation, I made friends with many of the Punjabi nurses, enjoying tea times and occasional sleepovers at their hostel. They were all far from their homes in the Punjab, and most were only a couple of years older than I was. We would sit together during the tea time break at the hospital, eating greasy *parathas* and sipping hot chai. There was good-natured teasing toward me, and I was the brunt of a good many jokes – some I understood and others fired off in rapid Punjabi so I didn't have a clue what was really being said. It helped that I had grown secure enough to laugh with them at my own language and cultural mistakes. Somehow it was so much easier in Pakistan than it had been a year earlier in the United States. Mom and I continued to visit women in their homes, our relationships growing stronger with each visit.

THAT FALL, I entered my junior year with enthusiasm, joy, and a boyfriend. Skip had come to MCS by way of Iran, and I loved him as much as any sixteen-year old can love a boy, perhaps even more. We laughed and talked for hours, holding hands in the dark on Saturday night walks along the road between our school and the tiny village of Jhika Gali. We began those Saturday evenings watching ancient 8mm movies from the National Film Board of Canada whose appeal was that they allowed us to clasp hands in sweaty, teenage passion under the cover of darkness. After the movies, we walked the mile to Jhika for *chai*, omelets, and *parathas* at our favorite tea stalls.

I also inherited a best friend. Nancy, best friend of my younger years, had gone to the United States for her senior year of high school. Before I even arrived back in Pakistan, she had introduced me through letters to Elizabeth. Beautiful Elizabeth was half-Scottish, half-Irish with blue eyes and a personality that could rule the world. We shared laughter and food from home, and if there was trouble to be found, we embraced it. We lived life in living color, ever fun and exciting, never troubled or dull.

Elizabeth was more of an athlete than I. Her legs were longer and she had a natural ability in field hockey and soccer. My passport to popularity would come later in the year through acting and, the following year, through cheerleading. Short cute skirts, pyramids, and catchy rhythms appealed to my love of dancing and love of drama. I loved being a cheerleader. My junior year I had just arrived back from my two years in the United States, and I didn't dare put my body on the court to be watched, much less evaluated by boys whose brothers had called me fatty. But in my senior year after a weight loss of 25 pounds I joined the cheerleading squad. I was thrilled the day I tried out in our large auditorium and made the cheerleading squad. I loved every minute of my cheerleading days.

Despite Elizabeth's athletic ability, both Elizabeth and I shared a hatred for gym class. Our gym uniforms were ugly green chemises worn over jeans or white pants. Sweat suits look like evening gowns in comparison to what we lovingly called the "greenie." The school recognized the need for physical activity but knew that it had to be done in a way that was sensitive to the conservative culture that surrounded us. The "greenie" was the solution. MCS girls of the 60s may not have been thrilled with the outfit, but in the 70s we rebelled. We sewed on ruffles and sequins, and experimented with various shades of green. The result was a variety of green chemises, still serving the purpose but with person-specific bedazzling that lent them a personality all their own.

A day came in spring of junior year when Elizabeth and I did not want to go to gym class. In truth, we never wanted to go to gym class. An opportunity came one day when we knew that Debbie, our beloved house parent, would not be in her apartment. Here was our opportunity. Our teacher, Mr. Murray of the Scottish brogue and kilt, would not be able to contact Debbie to let her know we were missing. So we went to her apartment to make fudge, planning to return to our room to eat it while our classmates sweated through gym class. The plan was foolproof, or so we thought, until Debbie walked into her apartment. We gave each other an "oh crap!" look but played it cool. And then Debbie said,

"Aren't you girls supposed to be at gym?" We had the grace to blush, and our guilty faces told the rest of the story. Debbie sent us on our way, but we didn't go to gym. We took the fudge to the prayer room in the basement of the hostel dorm, certain that no one would find us there. Twenty minutes later, Debbie stormed in to say the most vicious thing she could have said to us: "I'm disappointed with you girls!" We all loved Debbie, and none of us wanted Debbie disappointed in us. We took to the field with chocolate-faced guilt, the fudge sitting like stone in our stomachs. It was not one of our finer moments. It is a credit to Debbie's huge heart and spirit of forgiveness that she loves both of us to this day, and considers us dear friends.

While outwardly we were the rule breakers, in private moments both of us recognized that faith was a primary ingredient of our lives. We might not always live like it in public, but in private, we knew that we loved God and we knew that God loved us. We were quick to disobey, but equally quick to confess and ask forgiveness. Beyond the surface were hearts that were soft to God and to others.

ELIZABETH AND I both grew more familiar with the principal's office and, by default, the principal during that year. I was already well-acquainted with Mr. Roub. He was principal of my elementary, middle, and high school from the time I was six until the time I graduated. There may have been a year or two in there where he was on a well-deserved furlough and another favorite, Mr. Nygren, took over, but overall it was Mr. Roub.

Chuck Roub was a big man with a booming voice, strong presence, and a heart that embraced his staff and students. He was a leader in every sense of the word, and he used his leadership skills to serve the mission community with integrity and grace.

Through the years our small school faced almost all of the challenges that a large high school in the United States would. Although home churches and mission agencies may have wanted to deny it, we encountered drugs, smoking, revolts and rebellions, staff/student tension, suicide attempts, deaths, eating disorders, and more. All these took place in a complicated context – a small, Christian sub-culture in the middle of a Muslim country. It took incredible wisdom and sometimes just pure grit and determination to work at the school and believe in its mission. Mr. Roub had all of that and more.

Because he was in our mission agency, I often called him Uncle Chuck. We were like extended family and the auntie and uncle labels were used all the time. In the absence of blood family, we didn't need a Mister or a Missus. We needed something more, and the auntie and uncle title put more responsibility onto us, and onto those given the title.

I grew up knowing Uncle Chuck as principal of our school and as friend to my dad. At one point when Dad was deeply discouraged about his work in Pakistan, he wrote a letter to his friend. Uncle Chuck boarded an overnight train that took 18 hours to visit my dad for a few hours, just to encourage him, then he boarded the train back.

When my parents would come to Murree, they always visited, and often stayed, with the Roubs. This became more complicated in my junior year. I had all sorts of reasons to spend time in the principal's office. Smoking was one of them. As in most high schools, smoking was absolutely forbidden. But K-2 cigarettes, with a pristine picture of the famous K-2 mountain on the outside and ghastly, unfiltered cigarettes on the inside, were cheap and accessible.

But my conscience was strong, and one day I found myself in the Roub's living room making up a story about a friend who I knew was smoking. "What on earth should I do?" I asked. Uncle Chuck was a man of wisdom. He asked the right questions and quickly discovered that "the friend" was me. He gave me a punishment, but he did more: Like a priest, he absolved me, prayed with and for me, and sent me on my way. I never smoked again, and this marked the last time I was ever in the principal's office.

EARLY FALL OF my junior year, I received a telegram from my parents. Telegrams were never good news. We received them, and sent them, during times of emergency and crisis. Just as a telegram had informed us of the news of Peter Hover's death so many years before, so did my last two years of high school include two telegrams with bad news. Though a year apart, they both came in the month of September.

The first brought gut-wrenching news that my brother Stan had been in a terrible car accident in Turkey. Stan and his friend and classmate Paul Johnson were taking a year off college, traveling overland. The last we had heard, all was fine. They were expected in Pakistan in early September. The telegram brought news that they were both lying unconscious in a hospital in Ankara, Turkey. Because of visa situations, it was decided that Connie and Larry Johnson would go to Turkey first to care for both of them. They would let Mom and Dad know if Stan needed them there. The news spread quickly through our community, and prayers were offered on their behalf constantly. Memories of the year that Stan broke his arm emerged, and I was scared. Would Stan live? Would he have permanent brain damage? What about Paul?

Connie and Larry arrived in Ankara a few days later and found Stan concious, while their son still lay unresponsive in a hospital bed. Three weeks later, he too woke. The boys began a long rehabilitation process. They both healed and arrived in Pakistan a couple of months later. Miraculously, there was only minor residual damage. Once again I was witness to the fact that accidents and bad news were a part of life. You didn't let the news paralyze you – you did what you had to do, even when it meant traveling far distances to help the person who needed you.

The second telegram came in September of my senior year from my brother Ed. Sharon, his wife of only four years, had been diagnosed with a malignant brain tumor. The telegram was short – telegrams never could give all the information you wanted – and he ended it with Romans 8:28. I had memorized that verse years before, and it was a text that the missionary community clung to during any tragedy. Somehow we all had to believe, "All things work together for good to them that love God, to them who are called according to His purpose." How can you be twenty-five years old and be told that your wife has a malignant tumor and send a telegram to your parents with words of hope? I don't know. I wasn't the main character in that story. I was a bystander, receiving the news via telegram, thousands and thousands of miles away.

Ed was far away from us and from Pakistan as he went through that year. We heard news through the year – sometimes good, other times concerning. Surgeries and hospitalizations became part of his life, while on the other side of the world, I was finishing up high school. We would not see him until the summer that I graduated. Ed lost Sharon in the spring of 1981. He was twenty-eight-years old, throwing dirt into her grave even as his four-year-old daughter waited for him at home. All things work together for good.... all things work together for good. It was our own call to prayer – a call that we heard over and over through the years, until it was either accepted or rejected by the hearer.

PAINFUL GOODBYES BEGAN at the end of our junior year; seven of our class of sixteen left for their passport countries. I said goodbye to Tina who I had known since I was a little girl; to Margo who had become a dear friend; and to Elizabeth – my best friend and comrade. It had been a special year of bonding and boyfriends. Seven of us shared the same bedroom full of memories and secrets of the heart. I went into the summer of my senior year with a heart heavy with the burden of these goodbyes. It was a precursor to what the following year and graduation would be.

But I had been marked by resilience from the time I was six years old and crying tears into my pillow on the first day of boarding. This was just one more challenge on life's road. I would not let the loss of my best friends ruin my senior year. And I didn't.

I entered into senior year as queen of my world. Others had come before me, and others would come behind, but this year I was queen. The angst and rule breaking that characterized my junior year was gone. I found a place of security in my faith and my world. I had lost weight, I was a cheerleader, I was co-editor of the school newspaper, and I was popular. For a brief time, I owned the school. The year began with joyful expectation.

As the school year continued, I picked out my senior pictures and the yearbook quote from George Bernard Shaw that I chose captures the year: "*Life is no 'brief candle' for me. It is a sort of splendid torch which I have got hold of for the moment, and I want to make it burn as brightly as possible before handing it on to future generations."* This was my time and I would make it count.

In late April around 40 of us, accompanied by several staff, travelled to Kabul to represent our school at an inter-school fine arts convention. We would compete in debate, theater, music, and art, joining high schools from New Delhi, Islamabad, Lahore, Karachi and Kabul. I loved these fine arts conventions. Though I was left behind during athletic tournaments, acting and speaking were areas where I excelled.

This was not my first trip to Afghanistan. Our family had vacationed there periodically during my life. I remember tasting my first strawberry during a summer vacation, years before, juicy and red, like nothing I had ever tasted, instilling in me a love of this beautiful fruit. But this trip was different. I was older, my family was not with me, and this was our final school trip of that year. In a couple of months, I would leave Pakistan for the United States and a new life in college.

We boarded the bus early in the morning to begin the long trip down the mountain toward Peshawar. From Peshawar we wound upwards through the famed Khyber Pass, stopping for mouth-watering kebabs in Jalalabad. Late in the day, we arrived in Kabul and made our way to the homes of our expat hosts. We were housed around the city at the homes of various embassy and business expatriates. Our activities began the day after we arrived.

These interschool events were highlights of the year. We made new friends, expanding out of our small community to hear other ideas and thoughts. We performed plays and had debates, and learned new skills like calligraphy and water color. In the evenings there were special events and dances. Murree kids always had to sit at the sidelines during dances, painfully aware of our "weird" status. There was a school rule that prohibited dancing, some of us hated that rule and vowed to break it. I loved to dance and had already been punished in the past for breaking the rule. This was my senior year, and I was wise enough to decide ahead of time that when the final night dance came, I would keep my feet on the ground and kiss my boyfriend instead. It seemed a good compromise. There were no rules against kissing.

The decision that I had made so carefully and with so much thought would never be tested. On our second to last day in Kabul, in the midst of our performance of Thornton Wilder's *Our Town*, a play in which I was making my debut as the student director, school administrators entered the auditorium, interrupted the play, and herded us from the theatre on campus to the gymnasium. The gym was located in the center of campus and was less conspicuous from the main road. We were told that under no circumstances were we to leave the building; even permission to go the bathroom was restricted to two at a time. When my turn to use the facilities came, my high school friend, Sarah, and I peeked through a window and were shocked to see giant army tanks rolling through town. They were moving fast and purposefully, and we soon lost count of how many had passed. We knew something serious was happening and speculated quietly about what it might be.

An hour later, an important looking official came into the gym. He didn't have to ask for our attention. We were so quiet we could hear only our own breathing and, in the background, the sound of those heavy trucks barreling down the road. There had been a military coup. None of us would be going home as planned. All of us would be sent to the embassy houses closest to the high school until it was safe to travel. We were under strict curfew, and no one was to break that curfew. He finished speaking and we soberly lined up to go to various homes.

I was placed with several friends, and that was really all that mattered to me. All hell may break loose in Afghanistan, but be assured they better put me with my friends or they would have a far more difficult situation on their hands. Our sober and uncharacteristically obedient response ended as soon as we arrived at the house where we would be staying. It was party time.

We were unused to the joys of a commissary that supplied the latest in American foods even to a country as far removed as Afghanistan. Our hostess, Joan Fort, had the gift of hospitality and a well-stocked pantry full of cake mixes, chocolate, American peanut butter, and more. We became such good friends that when I returned to Pakistan, married with a baby, she and her husband, who had been transferred to Islamabad, immediately took all of us in. While Kabul was under military curfew and warplanes flew over and around us, we baked cakes and created a party.

That evening, more than twenty of us sat in the Fort's dining room and on their balcony, eating fried chicken and watching warplanes dive through the air. It was like a movie scene. I don't remember once being afraid. We were safe. We were secure. We were teenagers lucky enough to have won an extra vacation away from school, in a foreign country, eating commissary food. The gods were to be praised. Who cared that a country had been invaded, an ambassador killed, a king deposed? To our everyday world, this meant nothing.

I cringe as I remember my callousness, my ignorance of history and politics. This coup would be known in history as the "Saur Revolution," the revolution that paved the way for the Soviet invasion just one year later. A few years later, I was to meet my husband and tell him tales of the Kabul Coup. "It was awful," I would say. "There we were, over twenty of us in the house, watching planes swoop overhead and snipers shoot anyone who broke curfew." And then we found my diary and the truth was revealed. For in the diary, there is little about world events, and a great deal that speaks to the teenager I was and what I truly cared about. I wrote about my boyfriend, about my frustration with my boyfriend, about my friends, and about the cake we made and ate. I wrote almost nothing about the historical Kabul Coup.

As I think about third culture kids, and our lives between worlds, this does not surprise me. Instead, I think about what we saw as regular life – military coups, blackouts, wars between nations, constant movement, train parties. For us this was normal. Only much later would I grow to deeply regret not putting something substantive and historical inside the pages of the red-bound book modestly entitled "My Diary."

FAITH IN HIGH school was marked by occasional 'revivals' that swept through our small community, bringing waves of tears and confession. We confessed going too far with a boy, though none of us quite knew how far too far was. We tearfully confessed hatred of classmates. We confessed gossip. We confessed all of these things earnestly, heavy-hearted with soul-searching repentance.

At Sunday night "singspirations" we sang what passed for new and modern songs. "It Only Takes a Spark," we sang with gusto, "to get a fire going." "I Wish We'd All Been Ready," we sang, and quaked at the thought of being among those left behind at the Rapture. We sang "The Gospel in a Word is Love" in a round allowing the harmony to echo.

We were experiencing the first rudimentary precursors to contemporary worship music, and the new tunes and hint of a beat seemed to us a huge advance over the hymns of our childhood. We were oblivious to the pitiful theology, which would not survive, while the hymns of my parents' generation continue to echo timeless truths of the faith. But we were good singers, we loved to sing, and our self-taught guitarists led our worship with sincerity, if not always skill.

My hormones shifted, my verbalized faith oscillated, but there was a constancy to what I believed. My doubts were frequent, my faith was immature, but the foundation that had been set many years before had an immoveable, stone-like quality. Inappropriate touch, homesickness, intimate acquaintance with loss, the humiliation of beating – none of this had crushed my faith. God had not beaten me. God had not disrespected my body. Bad things happened all the time – they happened to everybody. Who was I to be immune?

I did question. Why did Lizzy's dad die? Why did a little baby die in a freak accident? The questions built up through the years, but at that time, the answers did not seem difficult. I willingly and purposefully rebelled in words and actions, but I never saw this as discarding my faith and my need for God. This Christian faith seemed able to take me through sadness and insecurity, through a lifetime of separation from my parents. I had watched as others who had lost far more than I had continued to believe. Carol Hover never seemed to turn her back on her faith. The parents of that baby girl who was killed so long ago didn't turn their backs on their faith. Instead, it seemed to me, their faith in God, their belief in his love, seemed to grow stronger.

When the telegram came from my brother, telling us the news of Sharon's brain tumor, I clung to Debbie, my house parent. I don't remember specific things she said – but I do remember her presence. I remember that we prayed together. I remember that she never spoke banal platitudes, but she was a witness bearer to what I was thinking and what I was feeling. Who was I, I reasoned, to not believe in the ultimate goodness of God when my brother, who had far more to lose, would accept it? These were some of the questions I discussed with Debbie during my senior year.

I know now that something critical was happening within me. My faith was no longer a copycat version of those around me. It had become my own. I was learning that it wasn't enough to know what other people believed, I needed to know what I believed. Maybe that is part of the mystery of faith.

Do any of us really understand the anatomy of a faith? Certainly it is the cornerstone of Christianity. But can we do any more than admit that its most important ingredient is mystery? That I was sensitive to spiritual things from a young age was obvious. But what propels a person to make the leap from a child's faith to an adult faith? What convinces one that they need God for each breath they take, while another discards God along with her childhood toys? Centuries ago, people asked Jesus to give them a sign that he was the Son of God. He answered them in a metaphor. Some believed and some didn't. I had seen more than metaphors of the existence of God. I had seen living examples of faith. Nevertheless, the holy mystery of faith still puzzles and disturbs me. But at this stage of my life, as each day brought me closer to the end of childhood, my faith grew more and more crucial.

The Bible, previously displaced by novels under the bedclothes, was now by my bedside. Its pages became worn with page turning, and the 'red-letter boring' of the past was replaced by honest interest and searching. I kept a black-inked pen at the ready to underline verses and write in the margins. I scribbled questions in the margins, and my diary now recorded less of 'boyfriend' and more about the God-Man, Jesus. I began memorizing verses and reading books on prayer – *Daring to Draw Near* – and on the Psalms of Ascent – *A Long Obedience in the Same Direction*. I underlined them as much as I did my Bible.

My final months in Murree were filled with joy, peace, and security. I was preparing to graduate. I had been accepted into West Suburban School of Nursing in a suburb that bordered the city of Chicago. It was a school that several students from MCS had attended, and I was excited about my chosen profession. Spring that year in Murree was glorious, a succession of picture-perfect days of sunshine and daisies. All of life seemed good and God was ever-present. I had grown strong and confident in my life and my faith. I knew who I was. I knew where I was going. The angst of previous years was past. Though I would miss Pakistan dreadfully, I would make her proud. I would make Murree proud. I was a daughter of this school and this nation. I wouldn't let them down.

The strength I experienced during that time was a gift. A few years later I would face challenges to my faith and upbringing that I could never have foreseen. But that spring, all I knew was that the God who had sustained me when I was six years old, weeping into my pillow on a bunk bed, was becoming increasingly real to me. My faith, born so young, was growing.

In a few years I would go through a crisis, wondering if God really existed in the United States. But for now, I was learning more of what it was to know constant faith through shifting hormones and circumstances.

This I knew, and I knew it well: when you're six and you wake up at five in the morning, away from home and unconditional love in a dormitory of seven other little girls, just as young and equally homesick and insecure, there is no one to comfort you. When you are twelve, and your backside aches for a week because of the beating of a house parent, there is no person to comfort you. When you question why dads and babies die in the middle of the night, there is no person to answer you. When you are sixteen, and you feel misunderstood by all those around you, unable to articulate your heart, there is no person to comfort you. When you are eighteen, and your heart is breaking at the thought of leaving all you know and all you love, there is no person to comfort you.

My faith was more than theology – it was a living, breathing entity. It wrapped me with a profound sense of comfort and love, and I knew beyond any previous doubts that God was real. I knew in the marrow of my bones, and the depths of my soul, that there was something greater than boarding school loss, stronger than the grief of goodbyes, deeper than the pain of misunderstanding. I knew that redemption was not just a theological idea, but that somehow it was more real than anything on this earth.

Faith was the story written on my life, and my life was witness to a greater reality. Day by day, I was learning more and more as my childish faith metamorphosed into an adult faith. I was learning that my story was witness to the God who made me in his image, ordained my days. He was the one who knit me in the womb, who saw my comings and goings, who knew my thoughts before they came to be. Like icons, their golden glow radiating off of church walls, my life was to reflect something bigger than boarding school, more important than identity and belonging.

Later in life, I learned to appreciate the use of icons as aids to worship in Eastern Orthodox tradition. I would learn that icons were windows to Heaven, the eternal reality. I would grow to love the rich colors of iconography. Later in life, I would learn that icons teach history, doctrine, morality, and theology. I would learn that they remind us "what we are and what we should be." I would learn that icons challenge us as we look at the lives of the Saints, the lives of those who chose to follow their God, their Savior. I would learn that icons bear witness to stories. I would learn that icons allow us a glimpse of the Kingdom of God.

But that was later. For now, my life itself was the icon. I was part of something bigger than myself, something better than all that surrounded me, something eternal. This was my faith story – a journey to something infinitely greater than myself.

THE LAST WEEK of my senior year we passed yearbooks around, struggling to write what our hearts were feeling with cheap pens next to black and white photographs. I reserved the best spaces for best friends and boyfriends, and retreated to quiet spaces to read their words. When I would re-read them in the future my heart would ache with longing. The week was a flurry of activity – concerts, awards ceremonies, dinners, and free time of lounging with our friends on picnic tables outside of the school. But amidst the flurry, we knew that this was all ending, and nothing could stop it.

The week culminated on a clear, starry summer night as ten of us walked slowly, one by one, down the aisle of the school auditorium. I knew every feature by heart. I had invited Jesus into my heart in this auditorium – several times. I sang in choir here, played piano for school concerts, giggled with friends, held a boy's hand, practiced cheerleading. It was this auditorium where we read our mail and watched basketball games. I had been in plays on this stage, playing the part of

Toinette in Molière's *The Imaginary Invalid*. This was where we had practiced *Our Town* for hours before heading to Kabul and the famous Kabul Coup. This was the center of our school, and its high ceiling and huge stone walls held the memories of a million events.

Elgar's "Pomp and Circumstance" echoed off the old walls of the building, saying to all those present: Here they are! It's their turn – their turn to graduate, their honor, the class of 1978. We had been to many graduations before, but this was ours. There were speeches, piano duets, and singing. As I sat on stage, I looked out on my community. I looked out and saw people who had written on my life. I saw my parents and my youngest brother. I saw my adopted aunts and uncles, my teachers and my mentors. I saw my friends and those who would come after me. In that moment, I saw only the good. The hard memories were not a part of this event, they weren't invited. The ceremony ended and our names were called individually. We stepped forward to receive diplomas with wild applause. Principal Chuck Roub presented "The Murree Christian School Class of 1978" and the processional began that would take us down the aisle and out of the church. We were finished. We would be leaving MCS and all that we knew.

Up in the cafeteria, a reception of punch, cake, and cookies had been set out, hosted by mothers of the incoming senior class. Giant crepe paper flowers in the class colors were hung from the ceiling. The reception line snaked from the cafeteria through the staff lounge, a space forbidden to students except on this one day of the year. These were my classmates' parents, and my parents' friends. They had seen me grow from bratty little girl to almost woman, watched me transform from turbulent pre-teen to happy teenager. They slipped envelopes into my hand – dollar checks, rupees in cash – knowing what was to come and how much I would need every penny. These were my people, my community. Each hug was long and hard in wordless goodbyes. Many of them I was never to see again. The magnitude of what I was leaving was not completely lost to me that night. Even in the midst of the goodbyes, I felt my throat catch. But as I look back I am overwhelmed by it. We left behind our entire lives the night of graduation. We said goodbye to all we knew. For the rest of our lives we would struggle to answer the question, "Where are you from?" We would rage at those who attacked our adopted country, even as we raged at Pakistan herself. Some of us would be accused of crying "every time a cow died in Pakistan." Others stoically moved forward, silent about the impact of being raised in another world.

In *Some Far and Distant Place*, my friend Jonathan Addleton writes poignantly of graduation night. It was another class, an earlier year, but the emotions were the same.

> "*By late evening, the crowd began to thin and, after a time, only we graduates and our families remained, talking quietly among ourselves. It was over, it was really over—there would never be a night quite like this, not for us anyway, an evening so full of promise and yet so tinged with all the sadness and inadequacies of adolescence. There was so much I wanted to say, so much I longed to do; but, as happened so often, I held back, keeping emotions inside that at this, of all possible nights, should have been on open display for all the world to see. I felt empty when I said my final goodbyes to people among whom I had spent almost my entire life, leaving in most cases without so much as a handshake.*"

Jonathan Addleton, *Some Far and Distant Place*

As for me, I went back that night to the cottage where we had set up our home for the past few weeks of summer. Suitcases and bags sat on beds and chairs throughout the cottage. It was beginning to echo with the empty place we would leave behind, and it smelled musty and damp, the effects of monsoon season already begun. Crying had to wait, there was still packing to do. But how do you pack up a life?

I stayed up to gather the remainder of my possessions, putting them into an old green suitcase, and finally fell asleep to the sounds of monsoon rain on the tin roof. The next day I would leave Pakistan and never sleep in this house again, never walk up the hill to catch the school bus. The final chapter of life as a child in Pakistan had ended. I was the baby turtle, making its way slowly to the sea. No one could do it for me. In order to survive and thrive, I had to do it by myself.

If the night of graduation had been near perfect, the morning was dreadful. We were all tired, both physically and emotionally. My parents were packing up and when they came back, I would not be with them. As my mom looked around Forest Dell, she told me later, "I was completely undone. I didn't know how I could do this. I didn't know how I could leave you behind." I knew none of this.

We were invited to breakfast at Auntie Connie's cottage, just across from ours. Before we got there, a vicious fight over clothes began. I was on one side, Mom and Dad on the other. I wanted to wear my cute jeans with a short, embroidered shirt. Mom wanted me to wear something that covered my bum, invoking the general rule whenever we left the house. "Wear something that covers your bum!" was a phrase said in every home in our community. We not only heard it at home, we heard it in boarding school. A "covering top," it was called. When I had planned this outfit – and I had planned – I was thinking ahead to Karachi, England, and beyond. I felt Mom to be seriously short-sighted in thinking I should conform to the norm. There was nothing normal about this day. My brain did not control my tongue, and I said some mean, nasty things to Mom and Dad.

In retrospect, the fight seems inevitable. How can you pack up a life without a fight? It's an impossibility. Ten years later, I would remember this fight when my husband and I viciously tore into each other over a cookbook in a Karachi hotel room, at a time when we too were packing up a life. Packing your suitcase for a trip and packing up a life are distinctly different. In the one, you put clothes and necessities; in the other, you pack your heart. Exposed and vulnerable, your heart sits in the suitcase and the even the most benign action can damage it. In that fight, my heart was damaged, mostly because it was already so raw.

My dear Auntie Connie gave us a break from our emotional morning by serving us a beautiful breakfast, and we forged a fragile truce. My boyfriend, Skip, and his father, Norm, arrived a bit later, and we packed my life into a small van and headed down the mountain. Conversation was minimal, it was too difficult to talk. Norm dropped us at the entrance to Islamabad International Airport, and we began checking in. Too soon, it was time to say goodbye. The goodbye was far more difficult for me than for Skip. He still had another year. He was a Senior and would enter with all the enthusiasm and energy that I had had a year earlier. I was the one who was leaving it all behind. Mom allowed us a public hug, which was incredibly magnanimous of her given the conservative culture where we made our home.

But the hug ended, and we went through security to the other side. The hot tarmac smelled like tar in the beating sun. I took one last look back at the terminal before I walked up the stairs to the door of the plane.

We landed in Karachi a couple of hours later. Our flight to London was scheduled for the middle of the night, so we made our way to the home of our friends – the Montgomerys. Mom used to say that Bob and Ruth Montgomery were the salt of the earth. He was as gentle as she was brusque. They had lived in Jordan before moving to Pakistan, and our families lived side-by-side for several summers. Joy Montgomery was my "big sister" in boarding school, and she had held me many a night when stoicism broke, bringing on waves of homesickness and a flood of tears. We had known them for years and were always welcomed to their home.

Auntie Ruth greeted us with *chai* and food, and Mom told Dan and me to try and take a nap. As we lay in their guest room, I looked at the ceiling fan and drowsily talked about Skip, wondering if we would stay together, if he would get another girlfriend. With complete confidence, my young brother said, "You won't," and turned away. I was wounded, and angry at his confidence, mostly because deep down I suspected his reading of our future was absolutely correct.

As hard as I try, I can't remember our plane ride to London. Those hours have been blocked from my mind, much like an old letter damaged with water. No matter how hard you try to read it, the ink has run together so that it is only a blur and can't be deciphered. I do remember London itself. We stayed at the Foreign Missions Guest House, a bed and breakfast designed to give Christian workers a clean and affordable place to stay in London. We had stayed there in previous trips through London, and once again we indulged in the hospitality of this guest house in a city that was hardly affordable on a missionary salary. The public dining room was always full of other travelers like ourselves, enjoying good British tea and cold British toast.

At the end of our time in London, I would travel on to Scotland to visit friends in Glasgow and Fraserburgh, while Dan and my parents returned to the U.S. On the day that our journey together ended, Dad wanted to make sure I had everything I needed. Impatiently I assured him that I was a grown up, I could take care of myself. In Heathrow Airport I hugged all three, then hugged them again. Last-minute advice from my parents felt superfluous. After all, I reasoned, I went to boarding school at six years old. I had been groomed for this moment my entire life. A final kiss and I turned and began making my way toward my gate alone.

As I walked away, their beautiful faces etched in my mind, their goodbye kisses fresh on my cheeks, I didn't look back. I couldn't.

"Amidst all this madness, all these ghosts and memories of times past, it feels like the world around me is crumbling, slowly flaking away. Sometime, when it's this late at night, I feel my chest swell with a familiar anxiety. I think, at these times, that I have no more place in my heart for Pakistan. I cannot love it any more. I have to get away from it for anything to make sense; nothing here ever does.

But then the hours pass, and as I ready myself for sleep as the light filters in through my windows, I hear the sound of those mynah birds. And I know I could never leave,"

Fatima Bhutto, *Songs of Blood and Sword*

My childhood in Pakistan was an extraordinary gift – a gift that is foundational to who I am today. What would I do if I could go back to those days? What would I have done differently? With 20/20 vision how would I have lived? If I could write a letter across time to that girl, the one who left Pakistan so many years ago, here is what I might say:

You are leaving Pakistan tomorrow. In the morning, you will have one of the worst fights of your teen years with your parents. You will only stop fighting because your boyfriend and his father are coming to pick all of you up in a van and take you down the mountain to the airport. You don't yet know that as you leave the soil of Pakistan your heart will hurt so deeply that you won't even be able to cry.

And here is what you will wish about your life in Pakistan, a life lived between worlds, between East and West, between Christian and Muslim, between Pakistan and America, wishes that you have grown into based on greater understanding and maturity.

You will wish that you had taken Urdu seriously. You had such a good ear for this language and a strong foundation. You will wish that you took advantage of this and gained the fluency that was a possibility at an early age.

You will wish that you learned more about the music of Pakistan, that you understood the ghazals written with beautiful poetry.

You will long to relive some of your friendships with Pakistanis, recognizing in the future the arrogance of your childhood as a little white girl growing up in the East.

You will ache to go back and apologize – to houseparents whom you were rude to, to classmates who have left the faith, to others hurt by your choices.

You will wish you had spent more time in the inner courtyards of your Muslim friends, chatting, cooking, and learning, learning, learning.

You will wish many things; you will regret other things.

But there are some things that you will never regret. You won't regret that early in life you learned of a God who laces your memories with grace, who takes boarding school tears and turns them into joy in the morning. You won't regret that you learned of this God through your parents, through your houseparents, through your adopted aunties and uncles, through Pakistan, a land you love.

You will understand that, though you were shortsighted, you know the God who delights in healing our eyesight, in restoring poor vision.

With all you now know, can now see, you won't regret that you are a third culture kid, with all the complexity and joy that goes with it. And you'll realize that 20/20 vision is reserved for God alone.

I LEFT THE soil of Pakistan in the summer of 1978. At the time, there was little research on the impact of a mobile life on children. The term "third culture kid" was just beginning to be used. The only task ahead of me was to go back to my passport country, assimilate, and succeed. I wasn't sure what that meant or what success would look like. Since I was going to nursing school, I suppose I assumed that it meant I was supposed to become a nurse. Oh, and get married. I was definitely supposed to get married.

I never thought that moving to the U.S. would be an adjustment. It was never mentioned at MCS. "Reentry" seminars had not yet made their way into the missionary or expatriate vocabulary.

I had certainly seen others leave. They usually came back with new clothes and stories to tell of their passport countries. I was mostly interested in the clothes. But I had never paid attention to the experience as a whole. I was absorbed in my world in Pakistan, and would not have paid attention had someone attempted to tell me what it was like to move to a country that we knew only through infrequent visits.

I had never heard of frozen sadness, of ambiguous loss; I had never heard of the grief sustained through the years through frequent goodbyes and distance away from parents at young ages while at boarding school. The research around third culture kids would not become mainstream until many years later.

But I know what it is now. It is sadness, frozen in time. At one point, I longed to express my grief, but it felt foolish. What was there to grieve? I loved the unique experiences that defined my childhood. Plus, my experiences were years ago. I have a different life now. I have moved forward. But in more honest moments, I realized there was grief, but it was hidden. I realized that being able to see the people and places I loved, even if it was just one more time, would be a gift. But with that I also realized that sometimes that is not possible. I couldn't go back to what was. I would always have an echo of *saudade*, that wistful longing for what no longer exists. Perhaps that is when I recognized that closure would be impossible. Instead, I would learn to be okay with ambiguity, be at peace with paradox.

And somehow along the way, being at peace with paradox happened. I grew to love living between. Many years later I would attempt to express it in writing.

Any third culture kid who lives effectively in her passport country has a moment of truth when she realizes it's okay to live here; it's okay to adjust; it's okay, even if she never feels fully at home, to feel a level of comfort in who she is in her passport country. To adapt doesn't mean settling for second best. To adapt is to use the gifts she developed through her childhood in order to transcend cultures and to find her niche in both worlds.

In all my years since, no one has ever asked what I left behind. Many have asked, "What was it like?" "Were you happy?" Hundreds have asked the dreaded "Where are you from?" No one has asked what I left behind. But maybe, a friend of mine suggests, that is the most important question of all.

> *So when she comes to you, don't ask her where she's from, or what's troubling her. Ask her where she's lived. Ask her what she's left behind. Open doors. And just listen. Give her the time and space and permission she needs to remember and to mourn. She has a story — many stories. And she needs and deserves to be heard, and to be healed, and to be whole.*
>
> Nina Sichel, *"The Trouble with Third Culture Kids,"*
> Morning Zen Blog, June 20, 2014

What did I leave behind? Everything. I left everything behind – homes and friends, sounds and smells, places and sights, all that defined my childhood.

There were only three portable things that I carried with me when my passage through Pakistan ended: my passport, my memories, and my faith. The passport would expire, replaced by one with new pages, and with it a portion of my life would be gone. The memories would fade, though some would revive through reminiscing and writing. Only my faith would remain. Like all humans who embark on a journey of faith, there are markers along the way, and we move forward – sometimes willingly, other times hesitantly. Sometimes we are screaming and other times we are silent, sometimes we believe and other times we deny. All the while, the Author of our story, the Writer of our faith, continues to draw us ever to himself. And so it is with me. The story is not over; the journey continues. The mystery of faith is not over. Some days, it feels as though it is still just beginning.

EPILOGUE

I HAD FORGOTTEN how long the driveway to the Holland Bungalow in Shikarpur was. Turning off from the busy road, we entered the gate of the compound. Once inside the grounds were calm and peaceful, just as I remembered. We walked past homes of three Brahui families who had lived there for years, then on to the large bungalow where I had lived my last two years of high school. The property had the look of neglect. The grounds were thick with brush and desert plants, and a bougainvillea plant was growing, wildly happy with no human to tame it. Layers of dirt had settled over the windows and thresholds of every door, and dusty footprints showed that a few others had walked these rooms recently. I peered into my childhood bedroom, a smile on my face. The same bedspread that I had when I left at age 18 was still on the bed. I gasped in astonishment. If this was not proof that this was home, nothing ever could be. Memories flooded my mind and heart. I couldn't stop smiling.

I was 16 and my older brother Stan had gone into my room and locked me out. "Dear Diary," he yelled out in a high voice, egging me into a scream of protest. He yelled, I screamed, and suddenly Ali Madad, our faithful, handsome chowkidar, bolted up the path with a gun poised – whoever was hurting Marilyn would pay! Mom's embarrassment at her miscreants was acute. With guilty faces and eyes, she made us go and confess that we had just been fighting. Ali Madad, gracious man that he was, laughed and forgave us, partially because his affection for our family, particularly my brother Stan, was great.

I was 17 playing my guitar for hours on the verandah during school vacation – picking out chords to a Queen song. I was 17 sleepily getting ready to go work at the Christian hospital as a volunteer caring for moms and babies who had no other means of care. I was in the kitchen and Arbab came with a beautiful meal of *saag* and *maani*, the aroma of spices making my eyes water. And then I was 18, saying goodbye for the last time. The memories tripped over my brain like a waterfall flowing over rocks, desperate to find their way to the open fall.

I was on my way to visit Arbab, my childhood friend. I had last seen her 23 years before, when my firstborn was a four-month-old baby.

As we approached her home at the back of the large compound, Arbab came running out, tears in her eyes. She began blessing me, over and over she uttered words, *"Allah mahabbat, Allah jo shukr ahay, Bismillah,"* She hugged and blessed, her hand on my head. It was a greeting of biblical proportions.

We sat on the *charpai*. I could not have stopped smiling if I had tried. My heart was so full of the best sort of memories, of hope, of thanks for my past, and of thanks for this trip – an undeniable and gracious gift.

The visit ended soon after the evening call to prayer. I wished so much that I had brought something, anything, to show my love, but in my haste I had come empty-handed. Arbab hugged me as though she could never let go, and I hugged her back the same way.

The ride back was silent except for the clip-clop of the horse's hooves as it pulled the *tonga*. Tomorrow I would head back to Karachi to catch a plane to Abu Dhabi, then board a 14-hour flight back to the United States. Our time was over too soon, but jobs, demands, husbands, and children awaited my sister-in-law and me back in the United States. We packed up under the harsh glare of a fluorescent light, a fan overhead, and music from the Hindu temple just steps away from the back gate blaring through our open door.

As the late night call to prayer echoed across Shikarpur, I lay down to sleep, my heart burning with those conflicting emotions of deep happiness and extreme loss. I fell asleep under the whir of the fan, a deep dreamless sleep where all of life made sense.

CPSIA information can be obtained
at www.ICGtesting.com
Printed in the USA
BVOW06s0846070417
480405BV00009B/277/P